LANGUAGE OF THE SPIRIT

99 Devotionals

Jeremy Dick

Bloomington, IN   Milton Keynes, UK
authorHOUSE®

AuthorHouse™
1663 Liberty Drive, Suite 200
Bloomington, IN 47403
www.authorhouse.com
Phone: 1-800-839-8640

AuthorHouse™ UK Ltd.
500 Avebury Boulevard
Central Milton Keynes, MK9 2BE
www.authorhouse.co.uk
Phone: 08001974150

© 2006 Jeremy Dick. All rights reserved.

No part of this book may be reproduced, stored in a retrieval system, or transmitted by any means without the written permission of the author.

First published by AuthorHouse 12/13/2006

ISBN: 978-1-4259-5225-9 (sc)
ISBN: 978-1-4259-5224-2 (hc)

Printed in the United States of America
Bloomington, Indiana

This book is printed on acid-free paper.

Foreword

When my son, Sebastian, set out to serve as a missionary in the LDS Canada Montreal Mission in 2003, I decided to write an uplifting spiritual thought to him every week. After two years away, Sebastian was in possession of approximately one hundred of these mini essays covering a wide range of devotional and philosophical subjects treated in a personal, thought-provoking style.

After reviewing the material, only ninety-nine were deemed publishable. Certain themes became apparent. Much of it is about language—the use of words, their origins and meanings. A key message of the book is how the Holy Spirit communicates by touching the sub-consciousness; inspiration floats up through the filters of the mind, surfacing in voices and images shaped by personal terms of reference.

As I have written, I have constantly agonised over whether there anything I can possibly say that has not already been expressed by other, wiser, more experienced people, and with so much more authenticity. However, I have always returned to the realisation that I have mine own life, my own thoughts, and I have come to know what I know through my own experiences. For this reason I write in the first person. While I may quote the words of many others, I am expressing my own thoughts and opinions, and reporting on what I have discovered.

Since over half of my life's journey has been as a member of the Church of Jesus Christ of Latter-day Saints, it is natural that a substantial proportion of the citations are from the Book of Mormon and other Latter-day Saint sources. This work is not of exclusive interest to Mormons, however, since many other sources are cited. Indeed, this may serve as an excellent way of gaining insights into Latter-day Saint beliefs.

You may not always agree with my opinions, interpretations and conclusions, but I whole-heartedly hope you can accept my thoughts as a provocation to re-evaluate and bed-down your own thinking. Your experiences may have led your soul to sing a different song; and yet I hope the chords I strike will have some resonance.

Acknowledgements

I apologise to my wife, Yvonne, and my children Sebastian, Timothy, Angus, Robin and Felicity for the hours I have stolen from them to create this book. I thank Sebastian for an excuse to write, and for his appreciation of my writing.

I wish to thank Kathryn Worlton Pulham for going the extra mile in her copy-editing. She made many constructive comments that have helped improve the manuscript no end.

Most of my ideas are those of others. My spiritual mentors have too been many to remember. This work is a small gift back to them.

Table of Contents

Foreword v
Acknowledgements vii
1 Language 1
2 Understanding 3
3 The Spirit 4
4 Holy Ghost 6
5 Revelation 8
6 Conscience 10
7 Conscience and Conversion 12
8 Free Agency 14
9 Liberty 16
10 Agency 18
11 Choice 20
12 Moral Agency 22
13 Freedom 24
14 Suffering 26
15 Being and Becoming 28
16 Action 30
17 Action 32
18 Will 34
19 Willingness 36
20 Habit 38
21 Sacrifice 40
22 Sacrifice and Obedience 42
23 Service and Love 44
24 Faith, Hope, and Love 46

25 Faith	48
26 Faith and Uncertainty	50
27 Love	52
28 Love and Law	54
29 Kindness	56
30 Honesty	58
31 Respect	60
32 Integrity and Sincerity	62
33 Integrity	64
34 Gratitude	66
35 Beauty	68
36 Steadfastness	70
37 Righteousness	72
38 Persecution	74
39 Pride	76
40 Indifference	78
41 Selfishness	80
42 Greed	82
43 Life and Murder	84
44 Vulgarity and Profanity	86
45 Idolatry	88
46 Materialism	90
47 Possessions	92
48 The Golden Rule	94
49 Ethic of Pure Love	96
50 Law of Restoration	98
51 Extrapolation	100
52 Reflexivity	102

53 Luck	104
54 Potential	106
55 Chance	108
56 Truth	110
57 Light and Air	112
58 Salt	114
59 Separation	116
60 Prayer	118
61 Solitude	120
62 Silence and Solitude	122
63 Praise	124
64 Order	126
65 Holy Places	128
66 Temples	130
67 The Temporal and Spiritual	132
68 Spiritual Rebirth	134
69 Spiritual Progression	136
70 Spiritual Sickness	138
71 Spiritual Survival	140
72 Spiritual Hunger	142
73 Spiritual Debt	144
74 Seeds of Every Kind	146
75 Balance	148
76 Perspective	150
77 Invitation	152
78 Discipleship	154
79 The Sacrament	156
80 Estates	158

81 Immortality and Eternal Life 160

82 Kingdoms 162

83 Innocent Suffering 164

84 Pain 166

85 The Atonement 168

86 Condescension 170

87 The Condescension of God 172

88 Opposition 174

89 Golgotha 176

90 Bitter Cup 178

91 Wrath 180

92 Change 182

93 Yokes and Chains 184

94 Mercy 186

95 Perfection 188

96 Grace 190

97 Healing 192

98 Fullness 194

99 Life 196

1 Language

The whole earth was of one language, and of one speech.[1]

Regardless of differences in the natural language they speak, those who live the gospel of Jesus Christ have a common language—the language of the Spirit. A dramatic illustration of this is found on the Day of Pentecost. Peter's audience was confounded by the fact that their language was no longer confounded:

The multitude came together, and were confounded, because that every man heard them speak in their own language.[2]

The Spirit has the ability to communicate to us at a level more fundamental than language, in such a way that its impressions rise to the surface of our consciousness in a form that instils a personal understanding that is shared with others who hear it.

According to biblical history, there was a time when the whole earth spoke the same language. Even if I choose not to take the book of Genesis literally, this idea makes perfect scriptural sense. Everything stemmed from the six people who survived the flood. The ability of the people to conceive of idolatry on such a grand scale as the Tower of Babel depended crucially on their ability to communicate. The most effective way to disrupt the work was to confound their language. It caused the people to disperse, and the building of the tower was thwarted.

Unity is not possible without the ability to communicate, in turn made possible through speaking the same language. More important than mere grammar and vocabulary is common understanding. It is possible to converse with someone ostensibly speaking the same language, and yet fail to find understanding.

While the Church remains multi-lingual in terms of natural language, it carries with it a single language of the Spirit. I can find unity with my fellow believers anywhere in the world through listening to the same Spirit.

The Spirit has the power to help us rise above our language differences and unite us around the one language "which [sur]passeth all understanding".[3]

---

[1] Genesis 11: 1
[2] Acts 2: 6
[3] Philippians 4: 7

2 Understanding

And with all thy getting, get understanding.[1]

The outcome of any serious research can only be to make two questions grow where only one grew before.[2]

The more I discover about life, the more I am aware of how little I know. True knowledge teaches me what further knowledge I should seek.

The same holds true wherever the human mind explores the infinite, such as in astronomy or nuclear physics. But I cannot let the limitations of the human mind worry me, or deter me in my quest for understanding. In all my getting I must strive to develop the kind of faith and humility expressed by Nephi when the boundaries of his knowledge of God were stretched by a questioning angel. He makes this basic expression of faith: "I know that [God] loveth his children; nevertheless, I do not know the meaning of all things."[3] His certainty of God's love for him more than compensated for the uncertainty arising from what he could not yet understand.

Without exception, the most truly gospel-educated people I know are the most humble. Arrogance is most usually associated with ignorance.

---

[1] Proverbs 4: 7

[2] Thorstein Veblen, American sociologist (1857-1929)

[3] 1 Nephi 11: 16-17

3 The Spirit

I was at college in London when I joined the Church. A few weeks after my baptism, I went into the student bar, ordered a pint of blackcurrant and lemonade, and leant on the counter drinking it. I can't remember exactly what I thought I was trying to prove, but the Spirit was about to teach me a lesson.

Along the bar counter was the college Anglican chaplain drinking a pint of Guinness. He knew I had been investigating the Church, and he had taken an unhealthy interest in my progress. Now he came over and asked me how I was getting on. On learning that I had been baptised, he proceeded to bombard me with a tirade of "anti-Mormon" concepts. I was completely unprepared. I left that place feeling upset, shaken, confused and filled with doubts.

I returned to my flat in Fulham. I felt miserable, and had no idea what to do. I eventually resolved to pray, and knelt down beside my bed. As I poured out my concerns to my Heavenly Father, a profound peace filled my soul. I stood up from the prayer completely reassured. I had no idea how things would be resolved, but I knew that everything would be alright.

Two days later, I went to the monthly church institute book sale at my local ward, the Hyde Park Chapel in South Kensington. On the stall, a booklet[1] by Hugh Nibley caught my eye, and I browsed through the pages. It seemed systematically to answer every concern raised by my encounter in the bar. When I tried to purchase the book, the stall-keeper said that he had no idea where it had come from, and that I could take it without charge. It was waiting just for me. The booklet I had found was a response to the particular anti-Mormon book that the chaplain had read.

I have kept that booklet to this day. It reminds me of one of the earliest experiences I had with the Spirit. I learnt that day that the

Language of the Spirit

way of Satan is misery, turmoil and confusion; that the Spirit of God brings peace and reassurance; that there is a being that cares enough about me to answer my individual pleas for help; that the Spirit of Peace is the vehicle He uses to transmit His love; that He works miracles in response to simple faith.

---

[1] *No Ma'am That's Not History,* Hugh Nibley, Bookcraft, 1946

4 Holy Ghost

"What is the difference between the Light of Christ and the Holy Ghost?" asked a gospel doctrine teacher. The ensuing discussion yielded the following understanding:

My conscience—the Light of Christ within me—is part of every human being.[1] It is the instrument of my soul that enables me to know good from evil.[2] In particular, it informs me of things that are wrong as I do them, or as I imagine doing them. As one participant in the discussion said, it is the cold hand that envelops an ignited heart to signal wrong-doing. It is the alarm that sounds on detection of any contradiction of deep-rooted values.

In contrast, the Holy Ghost is a being in its own right who actively strives on behalf of every individual. As a member of the Godhead, the Holy Ghost brings the presence of God to a telestial earth.

The scriptures tell us that the Holy Ghost "does not always strive with man",[3] but I should daily thank my Father in Heaven for the fact that the Holy Ghost does strive with me. The Holy Ghost strove with me before baptism to edge me closer to accepting the gospel when it came. The Holy Ghost filled the mouth of the missionary who met me on the street, and bore witness to the truth of what I was taught. The Holy Ghost continues to strive with me after baptism, *confirming* the truth, *clarifying* my understanding and *comforting* me in moments of uncertainty.

The prompting of the Holy Ghost is commonly experienced not as a "cold hand", but as a warmth around the heart, a reassurance, a comfort. At other times, the prompting comes as deeply planted thoughts surface through the layers of sub-consciousness in the form of distinct impressions that instruct, direct and warn.

There is a sense in which the conscience tells me what *not* to do, whereas the Holy Ghost tells me what *to* do. It "[teaches me] all

Language of the Spirit

things, and [brings] all things to [my] remembrance"[4]. It "[guides me] in wisdom's paths, that [I] may be blessed, prospered and preserved".[5] If I choose to ignore the Holy Ghost, the Light of Christ is my backstop. If I choose to ignore the Light of Christ, then God help me.

---

[1] Moroni 7: 16 , "The Spirit of Christ is given to every man, that he may know good from evil"

[2] Genesis 3: 5

[3] Doctrine and Covenants 1: 33

[4] John 14: 26

[5] Mosiah 2: 36

5 Revelation

The first car I owned was a little blue Simca with a 1.3 litre engine in the back. It was perfect for zipping around the streets of London. One evening at dusk I was doing just that. I was late for a church meeting of some kind, and was cutting across suburbia at exaggerated speed through a network of narrow streets. At one junction, I swung the car into a road lined on both sides with parked cars. As I accelerated along the space between them, I became conscious of very distinct, clearly audible words in my mind. I recognised the voice of my driving instructor. It asked, "What should you look out for between parked cars?" I knew the answer, and reacted immediately by slowing the car right down. Quite suddenly a child ran straight out in front of the car. My foot on the brake brought the car skidding to a halt. The little immigrant boy's hands came to rest on the bonnet. Our eyes held each other's looks of fear and amazement. That moment is stretched out forever in my mind. The boy's life was saved by a guardian Spirit.

The most astonishing thing to me about this experience—and others like it—is the powerful way in which the Spirit communicates with me. I heard a voice, but it was not spoken; it did not reach me through my ears, although it was as real as if it had. No, it emanated from a level of consciousness deeper than language, deeper than conscious thought itself. The choice of voice could not be random. The voice had to provoke an immediate reaction to the very imminent danger caused by my careless driving. The message had to be understood and its urgency appreciated instantly. The solution was to use a voice and a question utterly pertinent to the situation: Not "Excuse me, but did you know you were going too fast?" but a question that focused through reason and emotion on the danger at hand.

On another occasion, I knelt beside my bed and prayed for help in resolving a particular problem. As my head nestled into the pillow

Language of the Spirit

soon afterwards, another communication rose to the surface of my consciousness. Again it came in the form of a question; but this time I remember the voice as my own: "Why don't you fast?"—the advice I might have given another. I fasted from that moment, and the following day brought resolution. At other times, the communication has emerged as a peaceful and reassuring feeling, a bout of inexplicable tears, or "a stupor of thought".[1] All have the same origin: that deep-seated instrument of my soul that resonates with the Spirit.

This is soul-to-soul communication of the most intimate and caring nature. It is at once sublime and subliminal (meaning below the threshold of consciousness.) As Paul says, "The Spirit itself beareth witness with our spirit."[2] The Lord said, "I will tell you in your mind and in your heart, by the Holy Ghost . . . this is the spirit of revelation."[3]

---

[1] Doctrine and Covenants 9: 9
[2] Romans 8: 16
[3] Doctrine and Covenants 8: 2-3

6 Conscience

> *Labor to keep alive in your breast that little spark of celestial fire called conscience.*[1]

"Nobody will ever know!" This insidious falsity is frequently used to justify misdeeds. It is a lie that lolls at the back of the mind of every thief and murderer, promising freedom from discovery. God, however, is all-seeing. But even if I were not to believe in such a being, there is someone else who knows everything about me. I cannot escape my own mind, my own memory, my own conscience.

The closeness of the words "conscience" and "conscious" is perhaps no accident. Man's brain seems to have vast depths of sub-consciousness. Who knows what is going on in there? My impression is that my mind is storing away much more information than I am able voluntarily to recall. The veil seems to operate in my mind too; like the sealed section of the Book of Mormon plates, there are parts of my memory that are reserved to be revealed later.

However apt I am at ignoring my conscience in this life, it will be different in the resurrection. There my mind will carry a complete knowledge of my life as if still "in the flesh, save it be that [my] knowledge shall be perfect."[2] I shall know "even as [I] know now", and "have a bright recollection of all [my] guilt".[3] I wonder whether conscience is not a forward projection of the consciousness I will experience in when I stand before the judgement bar of God.

I believe that the judgement bar is essentially an exercise in self-assessment. I know what I have thought, said, and done in life. To the extent to which I have failed to apply Christ's atonement through repentance, "the demands of divine justice [will] awaken [me] to a lively sense of [my] own guilt", and I will "shrink from the presence of the Lord".[4] Note that the Lord does not banish me from His presence; I shrink from His.

Language of the Spirit

I am ashamed to remember a time when I was spurred into repentance by the realisation that someone might hear about something I said. In an over-spirited discussion with a group of friends, I said something appalling about a sister in the ward. Such was the reaction of the group that I realised straight away there was a risk that she would be told. Pained by the thought of the potential embarrassment, I went to her myself, explained, apologized, and sought her forgiveness. I was released from my fear, with my conscience paid up.

---

[1] George Washington, 1st President of the USA, (1732-1799)

[2] 2 Nephi 9: 13

[3] Alma 11: 43. See also Alma 5: 18

[4] Mosiah 2: 38

7 Conscience and Conversion

Paul is the one who speaks most about conscience, and he is surely the most qualified to do so. As a devout Pharisee,[1] he had a keen sense of duty that lead him (as Saul) to persecute the saints for their blasphemy, an offence which carried the death penalty by Jewish law. Subsequently, Paul's equally strong conscience lead him through so much persecution himself. As the Lord pointed out to Ananias—who was understandably very afraid of Saul—there was a certain irony in what was about to happen: "I will shew him (Saul) how great things he must suffer for my name's sake."[2] The one who had caused so much suffering for those who believed in the name of Christ was about to become one who would himself suffer for Christ's name's sake. Paul's conversion was a miracle.

Everyone's conversion experience is individual. When reaching out to us, the Lord with His perfect discernment can go straight to the heart of the matter. For me it was a simple question on the street that appealed directly to my state of mind: "Do you believe in God?" For the rich young man, it was the admonition to "go and sell all that you hast, and give to the poor."[3] For Enos, it was the words of his father "concerning eternal life, and the joy of the saints [which] sunk deep into [his] heart."[4] And to Saul came these interesting words: "It is hard for thee to kick against the pricks."[5]

What did this last remark mean for Saul? The word "prick" is translated from the Greek word kentron ("kentron") meaning a "goad", a pointed stick used to prod cattle into moving in a certain direction. A natural reaction of the animal is to kick out against the cowherd, but the length of the stick prevents retaliation. Once more, the Lord discerns the individual issue: for Saul it is a question of conscience. It is the goading of his conscience—albeit misplaced—that motivates Saul to persecute the saints. Despite the awful suffering it inflicts, it is hard for Saul to go against this sense of duty. Hence

Language of the Spirit

the Lord's compassionate remark, showing understanding the reason for Saul's actions.

Conversion from Saul to Paul was a redirection of conscience. Saul's weakness became Paul's strength.[6] The persecutor became the persecuted. Devotion to the letter of law became devotion to the Spirit of Christ. A natural man with a great sense of duty became a saint of great integrity.

---

[1] Acts 26: 5
[2] Acts 9: 16
[3] Matthew 19: 21
[4] Enos 1: 3
[5] Acts 9: 5; 26: 14
[6] See Ether 12: 27

8 Free Agency

At the heart of Jesus Christ's gospel lie the principles of agency and freedom. With Michael the Archangel, Jesus leads the armies of heaven in a great war[1] over these principles. As the Creator, Jesus establishes the delicate conditions of mortality to maintain them. As my Saviour, he makes an Atonement focussed on these principles. As my Judge, he will hold me accountable for my use or abuse of them.

As expressed by President Harold B. Lee:

> *Next to life itself, free agency is God's greatest gift to mankind, providing thereby the greatest opportunity for the children of God to advance in this second estate of mortality.*[2]

Agency and freedom are separate concepts. I might have agency, but not the freedom to exercise it. But I could not have true freedom without agency. Both are gifts to me from God, but in different senses. I have agency because I am created in his image,[3] and I have freedom because he grants it day by day.[4] Thus I have "free agency," meaning that I have the freedom to exercise my inherent agency.

Of course, an omnipotent God could choose to suppress my freedom, but this is not his purpose.[5] God is a free agent. God is God because he chooses to be God. President Joseph F. Smith explains it as follows:

> *No man is like God unless he is free. God is free. Why? Because He possesses all righteousness, all power, and all wisdom. He also possesses His agency, and His agency is exercised in doing that which is good, and not that which is evil.*[6]

If God wants me to receive his fullness in eternal life, then the only way is by allowing me to so choose. "God will force no man to heaven."[7] "God Himself will not save men against their wills."[8] This is the reason why Lucifer's plan of compulsory salvation[9] would never have worked, however attractive it seemed. He could perhaps have forced man into immortality, but eternal life requires the exercise of agency.

---

[1] Moses 4: 1-4

[2] *Improvement Era*, Dec. 1970, 28-30

[3] Genesis 1: 26-27

[4] Mosiah 2: 21

[5] "This is my work and my glory • to bring to pass the immortality and eternal life of man." Moses 1: 39

[6] Collected Discourses Delivered by President Wilford Woodruff, His Two Counsellors, the Twelve Apostles, and Others, Brian H. Stuy, com2: 297

[7] William C. Gregg, "Know this that Every Soul is Free", *Hymns of the Church of Jesus Christ of Latter-day Saints*, No. 240

[8] John Locke, English philosopher (1632-1704), *A LETTER CONCERNING TOLERATION* (1689)

[9] "I will redeem all mankind, that one soul shall not if lost", "Wherefore ... Satan ... sought to destroy the agency of man", Moses 4: 1-3

9 Liberty

I, the Lord God, make you free, therefore ye are free indeed.[1]

My Sunday school teacher enters the classroom with five tins of food. Two of them are identical, and contain beans. One contains chopped tomatoes, and the other two are wrapped in plain paper and marked "A" and "B" respectively. She holds one tin up and invites me to choose. I point out, tentatively, that by presenting a single tin, she is not offering me a real choice. So she holds up both tins of beans; I still have no real choice. She now holds up beans in one hand and tomatoes in another. This time I reach for the tomatoes, but each time I try to take it, she swaps the tins over. I feel I am being coerced into selecting the beans; choice is being denied me. When my teacher holds up tins "A" and "B," I find that I am choosing blind; I have no idea what the "A" and "B" signify. Only when she tells me that "B" stands for beans and "A" for artichokes do I feel confident enough to choose. I have tasted both beans and artichokes before, and I prefer artichokes. But can I trust her? To give me confidence, she unwraps the tins, and she's right: beans and artichokes. But before I can make my selection, she withdraws the tins, saying that I have run out of time; it is too late to make the choice.

Exemplified in my teacher's object lesson are the conditions described by Lehi that allow a man to "act for himself"[2] in this life. She refers to the 9th chapter of 2 Nephi. God's plan preserves my freedom by setting up the following conditions in mortality:

1. *I must have real options.*

Lehi says, "It must needs be that there was an opposition" (verse 15). Otherwise I am offered only one tin, or only one type of tin. God allows Lucifer and his followers to provide that choice for me.

2. *I must have knowledge.*

Language of the Spirit

I am able to choose only through "knowing good and evil"[3] (verse 18.) God has instructed man through every age, and imparted truth[4] sufficient to allow informed choice.

3. *I must have time and space to choose.*

"And the days of man were prolonged [...] and their time was lengthened" (verse 21). I have "time . . . to repent" and "space for repentance".[5]

---

[1] Doctrine and Covenants 98: 8
[2] 2 Nephi 9: 15-16
[3] See also Moses 6: 56
[4] John 8: 32
[5] Alma 42: 4-5

Language of the Spirit

10 Agency

The power is in them, wherein they are agents unto themselves.[1]

Lehi classifies God's creations into "things to act" and "things to be acted upon,"[2] and names man as being able to "act for himself."[3] What gives me the right to be an actor in this world? Where does my agency come from? I could take as given that I have agency simply because I am a child of God. My Father has agency; I inherited it from Him. But the agency in me somehow goes deeper than that. Abraham reports a vision in which he sees the inhabitants of the earth as "intelligences that were organised before the world was."[4] In reference to the same moment in spiritual history, the Lord declares to Joseph: "Man was in the beginning with God. Intelligence, or the light of truth, was not created or made, neither can be."[5] Furthermore, agency has its root in intelligence: "All truth is independent in that sphere in which God has placed it, to act for itself, as all intelligence also; otherwise there is no existence."[6]

I believe that agency is intrinsic to intelligence, and therefore agency is inherent in every intelligent being. The Lord tells Joseph Smith, "The power is in [man], wherein they are agents unto themselves."[7] I am my own agent. God maintains my freedom to act, but He is not responsible for my actions—only I am.

With responsibility comes accountability. I will be held accountable for my use of the great gift of agency; that is what the "day of judgement" is all about. Indeed, the very fact that I will be judged is evidence of my agency; the Day of Judgement would be completely unfair if those being judged were not responsible for their actions.

I am created "to act for [myself] and not to be acted upon"; but if I abuse that right, I will be "acted upon [...] by the punishment of the law at the great and last day, according to the commandments which God hath given."[8]

---

[1] D&C 58: 28
[2] 2 Nephi 2: 14
[3] 2 Nephi 2: 16
[4] Abraham 3: 22
[5] D&C 93: 29
[6] D&C 93: 30
[7] D&C 58: 28
[8] 2 Nephi 2: 26

11 Choice

There is an urban myth that goes something like this: On a long international journey, a businesswoman makes a stopover at Heathrow airport.[1] While waiting for a connecting flight, she relaxes in a terminal lounge. Purchasing a drink and a packet of biscuits, she sits at a table to read. After a few minutes, the she hears a rustle behind the pages of her newspaper, and looks round to see that a smartly dressed young man has sat down at the same table, and is taking one of her biscuits from its packet. Astonished at his behaviour, the lady asserts her ownership of the biscuits by taking one herself, and continues to read. Another rustle alerts her, and she is furious to see the third and last of her biscuits in the hands of the presumptuous stranger. She looks at him thunderously. Calmly, and with a smile, he breaks the biscuit in half, and hands her an equal share. Rendered speechless by this action, she is rescued from her anger by the timely announcement of her flight. As she walks away from the table, she fumbles in her bag for her boarding pass. There, to her horror, she finds her own packet of biscuits.

In this parable, the woman and man believe themselves to be in exactly the same situation: a stranger is helping themselves to the biscuits. What is different, though, is the way in which each chooses to react. And that is the point. What made the lady so angry? She chose to be so. How did the young man stay friendly? He chose to do so.

In the Sermon on the Mount, Jesus tells his listeners that they can always choose to act instead of react. Instead of "an eye for an eye" and "a tooth for a tooth" (a reaction to provocation), Jesus invites me to "resist not evil," to turn the other cheek, to love my enemies.[2] Such an attitude requires a highly developed sense of freedom of choice in our actions. I do not have to automatically retaliate.

Language of the Spirit

Behaving in this Christ-like way also frees me from the chain reaction that otherwise results from my negative reactions to others. If one "shall compel [me] to go a mile," I will resent having to do it—*unless I voluntarily* "go with him twain," exercising my agency to put me in control of the situation, freeing me from my own resentment, and possibly freeing the other from the penalties of coercion. Dennis Rasmussen explains it succinctly: "evil propagates itself by the reaction it seeks to provoke in others."[3] I may feel resentful, but I cannot lay the cause of the feeling on someone else—it is still my choice.

---

[1] I first read this story in a draft manuscript by Professor Terry Warner, who claimed to have read a version in the *Readers' Digest*. It is retold here entirely in my own words.

[2] Matthew 5: 38-48

[3] *The Lord's Question,* Dennis Rasmussen, 2nd Edition, BYU Press, Provo, 2001, p. 66

Language of the Spirit

12 Moral Agency

The gospel is marvellous in its simultaneous universality and intimacy. It spans eons of time and the far reaches of space, and yet pierces me to the very soul. The Saviour's atonement is infinite in its scope, compensating for every kind of depravity of mankind through a perfect balance of mercy and justice, and yet addresses the most personal concerns of each individual believer. The principle of agency is likewise all-encompassing, and colours our whole life experience. It instigated great wars in heaven and on earth, and yet influences the most fleeting moments of choice we experience minute by minute.

While agency covers decisions as to what to wear and eat, such are rarely moral choices. But there are real moral choices that I make constantly, in the form of whether to share or to withhold my love.

I have plenty of excuses for withholding my love from people, sometimes those closest to me, at other times colleagues at work or strangers in the street: The person has criticised me, or shown lack of respect; I am in a bad mood; I have to do something that is inconvenient to me; The person presents some kind of threat that speaks directly to my fears about myself or other insecurities. How often do I make such decisions? Many times a day, as I encounter people at home or at work, in the train or on the street. I choose to ignore the mendicant; to be over-polite to the ticket inspector; to be perfunctory to one colleague, and super-friendly to another.

From humble introspection come three realisations: firstly, I *choose* to withhold my love. That choice may be severely habitual, but it is still a choice. And I am free to behave differently. I am free to act—to assert my freedom—rather than react, which defaults from freedom as a sort of path of least resistance.

Language of the Spirit

Secondly, withholding my love is a *transgression*. Jesus said "Even as I have loved you, love one another." The Saviour never withholds his love.

Thirdly, withholding my love *costs* me dearly. Sharing a smile or a hug, expressing concern or sympathy, are multiplicative in their effect. Such choices enhance my own and others' experience of love. Withholding my love shrinks my experience of love. It prevents others from coming close. It drives the Spirit away. It propagates bad feeling.

These are the kind of daily choices that measure the extent to which I live the gospel of love, whose principles reach far out to the universe and deep into my soul.

13 Freedom

"I fear neither pain nor death."

"What do you fear, my lady?"

"A cage."[1]

There are worse things than pain and death. As Jesus said, "fear not them which kill the body, but are not able to kill the soul; but rather fear him which is able to destroy both soul and body [...]"; and just to emphasise the origins and destiny of him who is to be feared, He adds, "[...] in hell."[2]

The most prevalent influences of Satan touch upon my ability to maintain freedom, through short-term reduction in self-determination and long-term addiction. Consider tobacco, alcohol and other drugs: use of these substances would reduce my freedom of action while "under the influence," and tie me into long-term destructive behaviour patterns. Addiction to pornography and other self-focussed sexual behaviour is equally real. I see also habit-forming tendencies in people's relationship to material things: the lover of money, the work-a-holic, and the technology addict. Any kind of addiction amounts to an erosion of freedom.

God's commandments lead me gently away from addiction. Living the commandments requires me to master myself rather than let myself be enslaved by my natural habits. When David O. McKay says that "spirituality is, in part, a consciousness of victory over self,"[3] he is relating spirituality to freedom. Part of experiencing spirituality is to have a consciousness of agency and freedom. Thus I can take actions to maintain my freedom.

But not even a cage can fence in our freedom. In his account of experiences in Nazi concentration camps, Viktor Frankl describes how he discovered this inner freedom.

Everything can be taken from a man but [...] the last of the human freedoms—to choose one's attitude in any given set of circumstances.[4]

However brutal and limiting the external surroundings, he found that nothing could remove from him the inner freedom to choose how to react in every circumstance. Could he choose to feel compassion on his fellow prisoners as well as on the captors? Not always, but in striving to do so, he was an inspiration to both.

---

[1] Conversation between Éowyn and Aragorn in the film version of Tolkien's *The Lord of the Rings*, "The Two Towers"

[2] Matthew 10: 28 (see also Rev 2: 10-11 and D&C 101: 37)

[3] *Gospel Ideals* [Salt Lake City: Improvement Era, 1953], p. 390

[4] *Man's Search for Meaning,* Washington Square Press, Simon and Schuster, New York 1963, p. 104

14 Suffering

For I reckon that the sufferings of this present time are not worthy to be compared with the glory which shall be revealed in us.[1]

At times I am tempted to ask, "If he cares so much, why does the omnipotent God not intervene to prevent all innocent misery, suffering and torment?" There is a very compelling reason for Him not to do so: to intervene on the scale required to prevent all human suffering would seriously compromise the delicate conditions of this mortal probation. As President Joseph F. Smith put it:

God, doubtless, could avert war, prevent crime, destroy poverty, chase away darkness, overcome error, and make all things bright, beautiful and joyful. But this would involve the destruction of a vital and fundamental attribute in man—the right of agency.[2]

By the time the world was formed, a huge cost had already been paid for the principle of agency: one third of pre-mortal intelligences were lost in the war in heaven[3] because they chose Lucifer's plan of compulsion. The cost of maintaining this principle during mortality is that innocent suffering on a vast scale will not be prevented by God's direct intervention.

I find this realisation immensely motivating. An unimaginable amount of human suffering takes place so that I can experience freedom of choice. What am I going to do with that agency? Surely I must strive to make it all worthwhile; I must use my agency in the way intended, otherwise all that suffering will be in vain.

After discussing these ideas with a friend in a Sunday school classroom, I wrote on the chalkboard the phrases "doesn't care" and "can't change it." When I returned a few days later, someone had added, "Doesn't matter in the end." This is an excellent insight. I have to view suffering in an eternal perspective. However hard it may seem when I experience or witness innocent suffering, in the eternal scheme of things it probably does not matter. What matters more is the way I choose to react to that suffering.

> *Within the discipleship allotted to us, we are [...] to partake of a bitter cup without becoming bitter; to experience pouring out our souls; [...] to acknowledge—tough though the tutoring trials—that, indeed, "All these things shall give thee experience, and shall be for thy good"* [4]

---

[1] Romans 8:18

[2] Messages of the First Presidency of the Church of Jesus Christ of Latter-day Saints, (1965-75) James R. Clark, comp., 4:144

[3] Revelation 12:1-9; Doctrine and Covenants 29:36-38

[4] Elder Neal A. Maxwell, "Plow in Hope", *Ensign* May 2001, p. 59. Elder Maxwell quotes Doctrine and Covenants 122: 7

15 Being and Becoming

Believing, doing and being are equally important in living the Gospel. I must do more than simply believe; action must transform my belief into faith; and through action I become something—I become like Christ.

Jesus asks His Nephite disciples: "what manner of men ought ye to be? Verily I say unto you, even as I am."[1] The context of this statement is interesting: Jesus is saying to His disciples that they are going to be the judges of their people in the day of judgement, and so they had better be able to give the kind of judgement He would give; in other words, they must be like Him.

I may wonder what living the Gospel is helping me to become, but in the end I will realise, when I meet Him, that I have become like Him. The disciple John talks about the process of becoming like the Saviour: "it doth not yet appear what we shall be; but we know that, when He shall appear, we shall be like Him; for we shall see Him as He is."[2] Then in the following verses, John emphasises some qualities that I can obtain through living the Gospel: I can become pure, "even as He is pure"[3] I can become free from sin, for "in Him there is no sin";[4] I can become righteous, "even as He is righteous."[5] And in this last verse, John makes the connection between doing and being: "he that doeth righteousness is righteous."

James also talks about the importance of being "doers" rather than just "hearers", and echoes the Saviour's question.

> *For if any be a hearer of the word, and not a doer, he is like unto a man beholding his natural face in a glass: for he beholdeth himself, and goeth his way, and straightway forgetteth what manner of man he was. But he that looketh into the perfect law of liberty, and continueth therein, he being not a forgetful*

hearer, but a doer of the work, this man shall be blessed in his deed.[6]

Imagine trying to shave without a mirror; my shave is unlikely to be perfect. In fact, without the mirror, I may not even perceive the need to shave. The scriptures are like a mirror in which I can compare how I am now (my natural face) with a vision of what I could become through living the law of liberty that leads to perfection (my face after having "received [the Lord's] image in [my] countenance"[7]).

It is important for me to remember that the primary purpose of obedience is in the becoming through doing, rather than just in the doing alone.

---

[1] 3 Nephi 27: 27
[2] 1 John 3: 2, emphasis and capitalisation added
[3] 1 John 3: 3, emphasis and capitalisation added
[4] 1 John 3: 5, capitalisation added
[5] 1 John 3: 7, capitalisation added
[6] James 1: 23-25
[7] Alma 5: 14

16 Action

However well engineered my car, however powerful the engine, however skilful my driving, my ability to accelerate, steer, and brake depends on that small surface area of the tyres where the rubber meets the road. This is, in a very real sense, where all the action takes place.

The gospel of Jesus Christ is a gospel of action. He is "the Word," and He preached the word, calling me to be not just a "hearer," but a "doer."

> *Whosoever [...] heareth my sayings, and doeth them, [...] is like a man which built an house, and digged deep, and laid the foundation on a rock: and when the flood arose, the stream beat vehemently upon that house, and could not shake it.*[1]

Even the loftiest principles of the gospel must filter down to specific daily actions to be of any real effect in my life. When a lawyer asked Jesus, "what shall I do to inherit eternal life?" Jesus replied with a question, "What is written in the law?" and then went on to apply the law with the parable of the Good Samaritan, finishing with the words, "Go, and do thou likewise."[2] It is action that transforms my mere belief into the strength of faith. "I will show thee my faith by my works [...] so faith without works is dead,"[3] said James. Doing can be defined simply as letting my beliefs affect my daily choices, for I can "act for [myself]."[4] It is only through action that I truly engage in the growth processes embodied in the gospel. Such engagement brings understanding,[5] testimony,[6] and peace.[7]

Even the great all-encompassing principle of love only truly expresses itself in daily deeds. "Let us not love in word, neither in tongue; but in deed."[8] Action is central to the Golden Rule: "Whatsoever ye would that men should do to you, do ye even so to them."[9] James describes the essence of pure religion in terms of deeds motivated by compassion.[10] And Matthew reminds that my deeds are my passport to the Kingdom of God: "Not everyone that saith unto me, Lord, Lord, shall enter into the kingdom of heaven; but he that doeth the will of my Father which is in heaven."[11] The things I do daily are truly where the rubber meets the road.

---

[1] Luke 6: 47-48, emphasis added
[2] Luke 10: 25-37, emphasis added
[3] James 2: 14-26
[4] 2 Nephi 2: 26
[5] Psalms 110: 10
[6] John 7: 17
[7] Philippians 4: 9
[8] 1 John 3: 18
[9] Matthew 7: 12, emphasis added
[10] James 1: 22-27
[11] Matthew 7: 21

17 Action

There is a story told[1] of Joseph Smith and Brigham Young in which Joseph publicly scolds Brigham for many things that he has never done. In the middle of a priesthood meeting, Joseph accuses him of all sorts of wrong-doings in a tirade that lasts several minutes. At the end of it, Brigham calmly stands up and asks, "Joseph, what do you want me to do?" At this, Joseph comes over to Brigham, throws his arms around him, and with tears in his eyes exclaims, "Brigham, you have passed the test!"

What was the test? To be sufficiently in control of himself not to return evil for evil. Think of the reactions that the natural man may exhibit in such a context—anger, indignation, hatred. Brigham's response cut straight through all these kinds of reaction to focus directly on *action*.

On the Day of Pentecost, Peter and his companions preach the gospel to those who were touched by the visitation of the Spirit. Their response is to ask the same question, "What shall *we do*?"[2] The same reaction to seeing the Lord in a vision leads Saul the persecutor to become Paul the Apostle: "what wilt thou have me to *do*?"[3] This is a question that should be at the forefront of my repertoire of reactions—reactions to things I hear taught at church, reactions to things I read in the scriptures, reactions to reprimands from those I love, gentle or otherwise. It is the question that will lead me to real repentance. Through action I show my obedience, epitomised by the faith of Nephi: "I will go and *do* all things that the Lord hath commanded."[4] Through action I gain a testimony of my Father in Heaven's will: "If any man will *do* [my Father's] will, he shall know of the doctrine, whether it be of God."[5]

If I doubt my ability to do some things, or if things seem bigger than I am at any time, I would do well to remember that "I can *do* all things through Christ."[6]

---

[1] taken from a cassette tape by Truman Madsen, LDS philosopher
[2] Acts 2: 37, emphasis added
[3] Acts 9: 6, emphasis added
[4] 1 Nephi 3: 7, emphasis added
[5] John 7: 17, emphasis added
[6] Phil 4: 13, emphasis added

18 Will

Thus we may see

- *that the Lord is merciful unto all who will, in the sincerity of their hearts, call upon his holy name. [...]*
- *that the gate of heaven is open unto all, even to those who will believe on the name of Jesus Christ [...]*
- *that whosoever will may lay hold upon the word of God which shall [...] lead the man of Christ in a strait and narrow course.*[1]

Whenever I see the word "will" in scripture, I think of its two uses: constructing the future tense;[2] and referring to the spiritual muscle in my mind that enables me to act out my choices. This second sense is clear in many passages: "The voice of the Lord is unto the ends of the earth, that all that *will* hear *may* hear."[3] "They *will not* that [the Lord] should be their guide."[4] "For I *will*, saith the Lord, that they shall hide up their treasures unto me."[5]

In other passages, the sense is more subtle. When Nephi declares, "I *will* go and do the things which the Lord has commanded,"[6] he is using more than the future tense. He is declaring a certain commitment of agency to the Lord's service. In the great council in heaven, when the Lord says "we *will* take of these materials, and we *will* make an earth whereon these may dwell; and we will prove them herewith, to see if they *will* do all things whatsoever the Lord their God shall commend them,"[7] he is making more than a statement about the future; he is talking about the conscious application of agency in achieving certain things. So whenever I say "I will," I think not of the future so much as of my ability to shape the future.

And I read the scriptures in a new light. I think of conforming my will to my Father's. I think of Jesus teaching his disciples to pray: "Thy will be done in earth."[8]

---

[1] Heleman 3: 27-29, emphasis added.

[2] This use suggests that the future is something I can *will* into existence, a form of spiritual creation. Future tense is also constructed using the word "shall," which likewise could be viewed as having an emphasis on determination.

[3] Doctrine and Covenants 1: 11, emphasis added.

[4] Heleman 12: 6, emphasis added.

[5] Heleman 13: 19

[6] 1 Nephi 3:7, emphasis added.

[7] Abraham 3:24-25, emphasis added.

[8] Matthew 6: 10

19 Willingness

> *It is not requisite that a man should run faster than he has strength. And again, it is expedient that he should be diligent, that thereby he might win the prize.[1]*

> *To do what I can is all my Heavenly Father now requires of me. And it is all He requires of you, regardless of your disabilities, limitations, or insecurities. [...] We don't have to be perfect today. We don't have to be better than someone else. All we have to do is to be the very best we can.[2]*

I must do the best with what I have. But my best is not perfection; it is merely an expression of my willingness. Because I lead an imperfect life, willingness is what is expected of me. It is the grace of God through the Saviour's atonement that views my willingness as perfection. Through willingness I become perfect in Jesus Christ.

> *The Lord requireth the heart and a willing mind.[3]*

Willingness is all-important, to the extent that even those who died without knowledge of the Gospel but "would have received it with all their hearts"[4] will be redeemed. By contrast, those who choose not to accept the Gospel shall eventually "know that I am the Lord their God, that I am their Redeemer; but they would not be redeemed."[5]

There are those who would, and those who *would not*. With great passion, the Saviour repeatedly bemoans those who would not believe Him or accept Him: "how often I *would* have gathered [you] [...] but ye *would not!*"[6]

> *For behold, I, God, have suffered these things for all, that they might not suffer if they would repent; but if they would not repent they must suffer even as I.[7]*

This juxtaposition of the two "woulds" contrasts the Lord's willingness to redeem me with my unwillingness to accept Him. I understand his passion when I remember his vicarious suffering for me if I am willing to repent.

And so I do my best, mixing willingness with faith, diligence with recognition of limitations.

Do your best, your very, very best. Say your prayers and work hard and leave the harvest to the Lord.[8]

---

[1] Mosiah 4: 27

[2] Joseph B. Wirthlin, "One Step after Another," Ensign, Nov. 2001, 25

[3] Doctrine and Covenants 64:34

[4] Doctrine and Covenants 138:8

[5] Mosiah 26:26

[6] Doctrine and Covenants 43:24-25, emphasis added. See also Matthew 23:27

[7] Doctrine and Covenants 19:16-17, emphasis added.

[8] Gordon B. Hinckley, "Find the Lambs, Feed the Sheep," Ensign, May 1999, 104

20 Habit

> *That which we persist in doing becomes easier for us to do; not that the nature of the thing itself has changed, but that our power to do is increased.*[1]

I know that the muscles of the body work according to the above claim. The more I exercise, the easier it becomes to exercise. I start out by being exhausted after twenty lengths of the swimming pool, and end up after some weeks being able to swim forty lengths comfortably.

What I tend to forget is that the muscles of the mind have the same characteristic. Repeated patterns of thought are burned into the brain, and become easier to recall. After moving to a different home, I found myself driving back from my workplace to the old house on several occasions, out of sheer force of habit.

There is safety in good habits. I teach my children to clean their teeth before going to bed, to put their seats belts on in the car, and to read the scriptures every day, to the point that these things become habits. If I have not fulfilled the habit of kneeling before retiring to my bed, I will not sleep well; I feel instinctively that something is wrong; I have not wrapped myself in the comfort of prayer.

The safety comes from habits being hard to break. But if the habits are bad, this strength spells danger. Through repentance, I strive to cleanse myself of all evil, but I find myself struggling against the inertia of bad habits, which somehow encapsulate a residue of evil in me. I don't want to perform a bad habit, but I end up doing it anyway. Paul recognised this in himself:

> *For to will is present with me; but how to perform that which is good I find not. For the good that I would I do not: but the evil which I would not, that I do. [...] For I delight in the law of God after the inward man: but I see another law in my members, warring against the law of my mind.*[2]

I know what is right, but I am carried away by the sheer inertia of bad habit into repeating something that is wrong. Bad habits, however, are not an excuse. I can never give up the fight against them. Many such habits I will never conquer on my own. I will need the help of those who love me. On one occasion, a bad habit of mine was immediately and permanently conquered by a combination of three factors: humility enough to have faith in my Saviour, a priesthood blessing from my bishop, and a frank conversation with my wife—three people who love me. My salvation lies, if not in the overcoming, then in the persistent striving to overcome. The Lord says: "In the world ye shall have tribulation: but be of good cheer; I have overcome the world."[3]

---

[1] Ralph Waldo Emerson, favourite quote of Heber J. Grant.

[2] Romans 7: 18-19, 22-23

[3] John 16: 33

21 Sacrifice

At times, the Lord has required me to be willing to make sacrifices, but has always rescued me at the last minute. I believe this is a pattern that demonstrates the love of God for me, and helps me to develop my love for him.

When I stepped onto the plane that would carry me to Geneva, Switzerland, to serve as a full-time missionary, I thought I was "giving up" three things: my life's savings (family circumstances meant I financed by mission from my savings); my career (taking a two year break in the fast-moving field of information technology at twenty-four years old was surely a disaster); and the respect of my father (who was vehemently opposed my serving). It was the last of these about which I felt most strongly; my father was consistent in reminding me of the other two points. Yet I was prepared to do it. I felt good about a five-year plan that included a full-time mission, and I worked towards it. When it became time to commit to serving, I gave notice at work, and informed my father of my decision. Then came the real trial of my faith: I was summoned home from London to face the full force of my father's dry, logical argument. Oh how hard it is to live with the disapproval of a parent!

However, "ye receive no witness until after the trial of your faith."[1] Later the same evening, while under the blessing hands of my bishop, I received a strong testimony that the Lord approved deeply of what I was doing. The Lord found my willingness acceptable. I could not have known at the time that he would negate the actual sacrifice through very specific blessings.

During my mission, my grandmother died, and left me a sum of money exactly equal to the cost of my mission. My parents came to visit me in Geneva, and, after meeting the mission president, understood more about what I was doing; in particular that I was not there under duress. Finally, the day after I returned to England,

Language of the Spirit

I telephoned my previous employer for a reference, and he offered me a job. Within ten days I was back in my old job on nearly twice the salary. My father said, "You *have* fallen well on your two feet!"

I am humbled to be in the company of so many others who have been willing to sacrifice and been blessed accordingly. While I was willing, in a manner of speaking, to sacrifice my father, Abraham was asked to sacrifice his only son. He was willing to the end to do it. If was an act of faith, because he could not have known that "God [would] provide himself a lamb,"[2] and that an angel would rescue him at the very last minute.

The Lord requireth the heart and a willing mind.[3]

---

[1] Ether 12: 6

[2] Genesis 22: 8

[3] Doctrine and Covenants 64: 34

22 Sacrifice and Obedience

To obey is better than sacrifice.[1]

The Law of Sacrifice is perhaps the least understood Gospel principle. From a limited perspective, sacrifice is often considered in terms of being obliged to give something up, but this is not what it is about. The word "sacrifice" means "to do a holy thing", or "to make holy," and thus has a very similar meaning to the word "consecrate": "to render holy."

Joseph Smith taught "a religion that does not require the sacrifice of all things never has the power sufficient to produce the faith necessary unto life and salvation."[2] These words come from a man who ultimately gave his life and everything through his service to the Lord. But Joseph did not sacrifice his life just for the sake of sacrificing; he died in the act of being obedient to the demands of his calling as the Prophet of the Restoration. The same thing can be said of all martyrs in the cause of preaching the Lord's gospel and establishing his kingdom, including that "infinite and eternal sacrifice"[3] made by Jesus Christ himself. Some of Jesus' last words indicate that his death was an act of obedience: "Father … thy will be done."[4]

Almost by definition, if sacrifice is not motivated by obedience, then it is not sacrifice. In the absence of obedience, nothing is rendered holy, not least the person doing the "giving up." This is perhaps the motivation for Samuel's comment about obedience and sacrifice above. It is not what we "give up" that counts, but what we give that is the active ingredient in sacrifice. It only feels as though I am giving something up when I face opposition to being obedient, and when I have to adapt my will to that of God's. It is overcoming this opposition that purifies me, and qualifies me for eternal life. On the subject of giving one's will, Elder Neal A. Maxwell made this statement:

The submission of one's will is really the only uniquely personal thing we have to place on God's altar. The many other things we "give," [...] are actually the things He has already given or loaned to us. However, when you and I finally submit ourselves, by letting our individual wills be swallowed up in God's will, then we are really giving something to Him! It is the only possession which is truly ours to give! Consecration thus constitutes the only unconditional surrender which is also a total victory![5]

Whenever I think of sacrifice, I try to think of consecration instead; rather giving something up, I am giving of myself as an act of consecration.

---

[1] 1 Samuel 15: 22

[2] Lectures on Faith, Lecture Sixth, N. B. Lundwall, compiler, Bookcraft

[3] Alma 34: 10

[4] Matthew 26: 42

[5] Elder Neal A. Maxwell, "Swallowed Up in the Will of the Father", *Ensign*, Nov 1995, p. 22

23 Service and Love

The words "love" and "service" in the scriptures are almost completely interchangeable. Consider the following:

> *If a man say, I love God, and hateth his brother, he is a liar: for he that loveth not his brother whom he hath seen, how can he love God whom he hath not seen? And this commandment have we from him, That he who loveth God love his brother also. Whosoever believeth that Jesus is the Christ is born of God: and every one that loveth him that begat loveth him also that is begotten of him. By this we know that we love the children of God, when we love God.*[1]

One of the messages of this passage is that if I love my fellow beings, then I also love God. Compare that with:

> *When ye are in the service of your fellow beings ye are only in the service of your God.*[2]

I might as well read the scriptures as follows:

> *Choose this day whom ye will [love] [...] but as for me and my house, we will [love] the Lord.*[3]

> *A new commandment I give unto you, That ye [serve] one another; as I have [served] you, that ye also [serve] one another.*[4]

The word "service" rescues me from the temptation of thinking that "love" refers only to feelings. A loving act is, almost by definition, an act of service, since if it does not truly benefit someone, then how can it be an act of love? But the connection goes deeper than that. It is by rendering service that we propagate the Lord's love for his children. When I feel the Saviour's love for me, it is almost always through service that others render to me. And a genuine act of service never feels like service to either the giver or the receiver; it is never humiliating, but always healing.

However, it is not so much the service that others offer me that heals my soul; it is rather the service I render to others that draws me out of myself. The Saviour said it, as always, so much more succinctly:

> *He that findeth his life shall lose it; and he that loseth his life for my sake shall find it.*[5]

And this reminder:

> *Greater [service doth] no man than this, that a man lay down his life for his friends.*[6]

---

[1] 1 John 4: 20 - 5: 2
[2] Mosiah 2: 17
[3] Joshua 24: 15
[4] John 13: 34
[5] Matthew 10: 39
[6] John 14: 13

Language of the Spirit

24 Faith, Hope, and Love

And now abideth faith, hope, charity, these three; but the greatest of these is charity.[1]

Of all principles, faith, hope, and love are the hardest to pin down and define. Perhaps one reason for this difficulty is that they are all intangible qualities of the "inner man." They make the difference between the "natural man" and the "saint."[2]

Another commonality among these three qualities is that they are overwhelmingly positive in nature. Faith replaces doubt, hope expunges despair, and love overcomes fear. Bitterness, hatred, and other negative sentiments have no place in a life filled with the Spirit.

Faith influences the past, present, and future; it motivates my present actions, helps me to interpret the past, and gives me hope for the future. Thus hope is related to faith. As Mormon asks, "How is it that ye can attain unto faith, save ye shall have hope? And what is it that ye shall hope for? [...]", and then answers "ye shall have hope through the atonement of Christ and the power of his resurrection, to be raised unto life eternal, and this because of your faith in him according to the promise."[3]

I believe the promises contained in covenants made with my Father in Heaven; I have faith in the atoning power of Jesus Christ; I can therefore "with a surety hope for a better world, yea, even a place at the right hand of God."[4] Thus faith leads to hope, but hope gives positive feedback to faith. It is precisely this hope of a better world that "maketh an anchor to the souls of men, which would make them sure and steadfast, always abounding in good works, being lead to glorify God."[4] In other words, the very existence of this element of hope makes me strive all the harder to express my faith through good works.

Paul hints that faith and hope are qualities especially relevant to the conditions of this mortal life, a time when doubt and uncertainty reign. "For now we see through a glass, darkly; [...] I know in part" he explains. But after this life, when all is revealed, there will be certainty, and fullness of knowledge. "Then we shall see face to face" and "I shall know even as I am known."[5] Faith will be different in that better world, when in the presence of God.

However, love is the principle that endures unchanged through the major milestones of our existence. Love motivated the Plan of Salvation in the pre-mortal courts; love is the central message of the gospel in earth; and love reigns in the glorious kingdom of God. That's why, Paul explains, of faith, hope, and love, "the greatest of these is [love]."

Faith is my spring-board; hope is my vision; love is my reason why.

---

[1] 1 Corithians 13: 13
[2] See Mosiah 3: 19
[3] Moroni 7: 40-41
[4] Ether 12: 4
[5] 1 Corinthians 13: 12

25 Faith

> *Through faith we understand that the worlds were framed by the word of God, so that things which are seen were not made of things which do appear.*[1]

Faith has many facets. It is expressed in terms of love, trust, obedience, and hope, always in the face of uncertainty. Paul characterises the essence of faith as "the [assurance] of things hoped for, the evidence of things not seen."[2]

What kinds of things are not evident to me? What kinds of uncertainty do I face? There are things of the past shrouded in the mysteries of history; there are things of the present veiled from the view of mortals; there are things of the future beyond natural sight. Each of these categories brings my love, trust, obedience and hope to play in different ways.

It is in the last category—the things of the future—that the creative person plays. Every act of creation is an act of faith, for the creator starts by imagining the thing before it is apparent. Conception in the mind's eye gives the power to bring something worthwhile into being. Without the ability to imagine—to create an assurance and evidence of things not yet apparent—nobody would be motivated to create. Paul understands the power of this kind of faith. By direct reference to the Greek, the verse cited above might be rendered as:

> *We understand that the worlds were formed by the word of God through faith, so that things which are visible were brought into being from things which were invisible.*[3]

God used faith to create the universe. I could not begin to imagine such a creation. It is marvellous enough to contemplate and discover the world as it is now apparent around me; but to have imagined it before it was, that would be too great an act of faith for my limited knowledge and experience.

Indeed, the greater my knowledge and experience, the greater my ability to imagine, and thus the greater the power of faith I can call upon. God's ability to organise the universe, spiritually and then physically, was only possible through the degree of knowledge He possesses. Nevertheless, faith was used in the very act of creation. To exercise faith in this way is a God-like, God-given ability.

---

[1] Hebrews 11: 3

[2] Hebrews 11: 1

[3] Hebrews 11: 3 rendered by the author

26 Faith and Uncertainty

> *What is faith? Faith exists when absolute confidence in that which we cannot see combines with action that is in absolute conformity to the will of our Heavenly Father. Without all three – first, absolute confidence; second, action; and third, absolute conformity – without these three all we have is a counterfeit, a weak and watered-down faith.*[1]

Faith is what helps me to cope with the uncertainties of this life – not knowing exactly how, or why, or when. In a world of non-absolutes, I can anchor my hopes, desires and expectations in those things I can master: my own confidence in a loving Heavenly Father; my own power of action; my own choice to conform in absolute obedience to His will. Adam was obedient in performing sacrifices without knowing exactly *why*, but that God commanded it.[2] Nephi journeyed into Jerusalem to retrieve the brass plates without knowing exactly *how*, but that is was possible.[3] Paul was firm in his belief that things would work out without knowing exactly *when*.[4]

Another example of faith in the face of uncertainty is the "but if not" attitude of Shadrach, Meshach and Abednego when they were to be thrown into the furnace:

> *If it be so, our God whom we serve is able to deliver us from the burning fiery furnace, and he will deliver us out of thine hand, O king. But if not, be it known unto thee, O king, that we will not serve thy gods, nor worship the golden image which thou hast set up.*[5]

These are basic expressions of faith: an absolute confidence that leads to action founded on absolute obedience.

---

[1] Elder Joseph B. Wirthlin, "Shall He Find Faith in the Earth?", *Ensign* Nov 2002, p. 83

[2] Moses 4: 6

[3] 1 Nephi 3: 7

[4] Romans 8: 28

[5] Daniel 3: 17-18, emphasis added

27 Love

When you ask, "Do you love me?" I might ask you what you mean. I do not intend any disrespect; rather, I am motivated by a deep respect for love, and a desire to understand it. Love is a complex thing, and sometimes requires a complex answer. You may be asking me one of several things, including:

- Do I have feelings of love for you?
- Do I do things that express love for you?
- Am I committed to you?

To each of these I must answer, "Not all of the time," because I am imperfect, and sometimes I feel distant, out of touch, and disconnected.

Love is both a verb and a noun. Love is manifest in deeds motivated by *feelings*, and in feelings evoked by deeds. My feelings are nothing if not connected to action. And yet somehow the feelings make my actions *love*. It is the motivation of love that allows me to do things "with real intent of heart."[1] Feelings are fickle things. Sometimes I think I cannot control what I feel—that my feelings of love for you come unbidden—that I have not chosen to love you, but that love for you has chosen me. At other times, I consciously choose to love you by doing something for you despite my feelings, and then loving feelings flood my soul. There are acts that create love.

Some would say:

> *Love is a verb; love is something you do. Love—the feeling—is the result, the fruit, of love. [...] If love is truly a verb [...] then you can do something about it. But if love is just a feeling, you feel almost helpless because you cannot control your feelings. Ultimately, your feelings are a function of your actions.*[2]

Language of the Spirit

Others would say "loving is not a behaviour at all; it is a quality of the heart and mind."[3] By this they mean that love cannot be recognised purely by my actions, but by my motivation for those actions. And yet motivation is only motivation in the presence of action.

And so, dear Lord and Saviour, do I love you? You have said, "If ye love me, keep my commandments. And I will pray the Father, and he shall give you another Comforter [...] the Spirit of truth"[4] [...] the greatest feelings of love.

Feelings and actions feed each other. Love is when feelings and actions grow towards complete joy. At first the feeling is just a "desire to believe,"[5] but through action it grows until I have "felt to sing the song of redeeming love."[6]

---

[1] Moroni 7: 5-9

[2] Stephen R. Covey, *"Love Enough for All"*, in *Handbook for the Heart*, Carlson and Shield, Editors, 1998, p. 60

[3] Hugh and Gayle Prather, *"God is Love"*, ibid., p. 85

[4] John 14: 15-17

[5] Alma 32: 27

[6] Alma 5: 26

28 Love and Law

One of the Pharisees asked Jesus which of all the commandments was the greatest. He answered by saying that two commandments stood equal in importance:

- "Thou shalt *love the Lord thy God* with all thy heart, and with all thy soul, and with all thy mind."
- "Thou shalt *love thy neighbour* as thyself."

And then these telling words, "on these two hang all the law and the prophets."[1]

The "law" (the Torah, or five books of Moses) and the "prophets" (the remainder of the Old Testament) refer to the major parts of the Jewish scriptures. I understand the expression "to hang" in this context to mean that all of scripture is subsumed by the principle of love; or in other words, every commandment is a description of one way I can show my love for God or for my fellow men.

For example, take "tithes and offerings."[2] Through paying tithing, I express my love for God by "[confessing] his hand in all things,"[3] for He surely does not need my money, but He does require me to recognise Him as the source of all my blessings. Through paying fast offerings, however, I am expressing my love for my fellow beings, for these funds are used to support those in need. These two expressions of love are not, of course, unrelated. As John says, "that he who loveth God love his brother also,"[4] and "by this we know that we love the children of God, when we love God."[5]

The Lord has said, "It is not meet that I should command in all things."[6] This is partly because it would not be possible to write commandments to cover every possible situation, to avoid every possible sin,[7] to describe every possible way of expressing love, and partly because I need to learn to govern myself. I believe that as I come to understand the commandments, I will be able to recognise the principle of love that underlies each, and so progress to the point where using the principle of love, I can govern myself without needing explicitly to be commanded.

---

[1] Matthew 22: 35-40, emphasis added (see also Mark 12: 28-31)

[2] Malachi 3: 8

[3] Doctrine and Covenants 59: 21

[4] 1 John 4: 21

[5] 1 John 5: 2

[6] Doctrine and Covenants 58: 26

[7] Mosiah 4: 29

29 Kindness

Travelling by train to London one morning, I felt hemmed in by crowds of other passengers. I looked critically at those around me. So many had body piercings, died hair, weird and immodest clothing, or ear phones playing aggressive music. I felt as though I was on a *Star Wars* set. Then, as I got off, and watched the hoards pouring from the train, I was overcome by a wave of compassion. With so many people in such a small space, no wonder some seek a means of being different, of standing out. A had brief glimpse of their pain and their struggles, and I regretted my unkind feelings.

The word "kindness" refers in one sense to the natural feelings of love we have to those who are of the same *kind* as ourselves. Nowhere is natural love stronger than in the kindness a mother feels for her children, who are quintessentially of her kind. Indeed, the German word for children, "Kinder"[1] has the same origins.

Of course, I should not use the concept of "kind" to be exclusive; I should be kind to *everyone*, not just my children, my family, my fellow countrymen, or fellow church members. Indeed, every human being is one of God's "Kinder." I should not forget the universal sibling-ship of mankind.

Compassion is the key for returning blessing in response to unkindness, for often unkindness is merely an expression of negative self-feelings. I know when I entertain unkind feelings towards my wife or my children, it is always because of struggles I am having with myself. So I say to my family, if ever I am unkind or angry with you, please don't blame yourself, but rather have compassion on me for the turmoil inside of me. And I should have such compassion towards others. I must learn to be so much the master of myself that I can see through the emotion of the moment and have compassion for the needs of the other, regardless of his or her apparent unkindness towards me.

Language of the Spirit

Love your enemies, bless them that curse you, do good to them that hate you, and pray for them that despitefully use you, and persecute you; that ye may be the children of your Father which is in heaven. [...] For if ye love them which love you, what reward have ye? [...] And if ye salute your brethren only, what do ye more than others?[2]

Everybody is a *Kinder* of Heavenly Father, and deserves our kindness, even those we class as our enemies. Not agreeing with them does not mean we should be unkind. If we are kind to our kind only, what difference are we making? And such was my momentary insight at Paddington Station: Christ's all-inclusive compassion encompasses those I deem to be the weirdest around me. They are my kind after all.

---

[1] As in "Kindergarten" and "Kinder Egg"
[2] Matthew 5:44-47

30 Honesty

And they were distinguished for their zeal towards God, and also towards men; for they were perfectly honest and upright in all things[1]

When I was thirteen years old, I was caught shoplifting. I stole a 5p bar of Cadbury's chocolate from a supermarket near school. Fortunately the shopkeeper didn't call the police, but went to the head master. My parents were summoned. There were tears all round. I went to see the shopkeeper to apologise. That dishonest act was actually the tip of an iceberg. To hide my habit, I had already constructed a complex web of lies. On this occasion, I lied to my parents and the school that it was the first time I had done it. I lied to protect my brother, who had been involved in previous shop-lifting with me. We were in different boarding schools at the time, so I wrote to him to tell him what I had said, so that he could corroborate with my deception.

For the first time in my life, I experienced the anxiety that goes with being dishonest. I had written the letter, and posted it, but my anxiety played tricks on me. It kept me awake at night. Had I really remembered to post it? Had I put a stamp on the letter? Would someone else read it?

I did not shop-lift out of need, but out of *compulsion*. The web of lies was motivated by *fear* and *pride*—fear of humiliation, fear of losing the love of my parents. These things, I was later to discover, are the hallmarks of Satan who as "the father of lies"[2] had "become miserable forever" and "[seeks] also the misery of all mankind."

Life in the company of Satan is the exact opposite of life with the Spirit, the Comforter, who brings peace and joy to reign in the heart. Through honesty with myself, honesty with man, and honesty with God, and through the principles of faith and repentance, I free myself from the need to weave chains of deception, which eventually bind

Language of the Spirit

me. From Alma's advice to his son Corianton, I learn that "[I] cannot hide [my] crimes from God."[3]

Mortal life is, in part, about learning and being tested to see if we can voluntarily live an honest life away from the direct influence of being in the presence of God. Nephi, the son of Helaman, makes this comparison between the honest and the dishonest: "Instead of laying up for yourselves treasures in heaven [...] ye are heaping up for yourselves wrath against the day of judgement."[4]

As a follower of the light of Christ, I should be known for my honesty, "distinguished for [my] zeal," honesty and uprightness.[5]

---

[1] Alma 27: 27
[2] 2 Nephi 2: 18
[3] Alma 39: 8
[4] Helaman 8: 25
[5] Alma 27: 27

31 Respect

Ye shall not esteem one flesh above another, or one man shall not think himself above another.[1]

If ye fulfil the royal law according to the scripture, Thou shalt love thy neighbour as thyself, ye do well: but if ye have respect to persons, ye commit sin.[2]

When I was a student in London, I often travelled back and forth to my family home in Reading. One fine Saturday (July 2nd 1977) I was standing in Reading station to return to college. The sun was shining. I was wearing typical student apparel: hair over my ears, faded jeans, scruffy tee-shirt sporting an irreverent slogan of some kind, and carrying my belongings in a plastic carrier bag. I was in the middle of eating a choc-ice, which was somehow smeared all over my face and hands. Even my father would have been ashamed to be associated with me.

Then I spied a smartly-dressed gentleman, and he had spotted me. It was Joseph Hampsted, our Regional Representative (equivalent to today's Area Authority), dressed in an immaculate pin-striped suit, carrying a sleek black brief-case. Without a moment's hesitation, he greeted me, shook my hand, ambivalent to its stickiness, grubbiness, scruffiness, and said, "Come, we shall travel together!"

I imagine that he had a first-class ticket, but he sat with me in standard class, and we talked all the way to London. He was not the least bit embarrassed to travel with me. What other than the gospel would bring two such together? Some time later, Elder Hampsted gave a sacrament meeting address in the Hyde Park Ward. He started his talk in an unusual way, by quoting the scripture, "I am no respecter of persons."[3] I felt like standing up in the middle of the meeting, and shouting "Hear, hear!"

Language of the Spirit

I am so often caught up in the way the world would judge others—by social class, by wealth, by the clothes they wear, by the way they speak. These are barriers to my being able to see through the apparent to the intrinsic—to cut to the chase, and value all others as equals, as siblings, as susceptible, as insecure and as vulnerable as I.

Jesus, as always, is my great example. He spoke unashamedly to outcasts—lepers, foreigners, adulterers, and tax collectors—as well as to the apparently "respectable." In some cases, we know what effect this had on the individuals concerned.

Jesus has also touched me through his disciple, Joseph Hampsted, who unashamedly showed me respect. Who knows what effect this simple example had on the direction of my life?

---

[1] Mosiah 23: 7

[2] James 2: 8-9

[3] Doctrine and Covenants 1: 35

32 Integrity and Sincerity

Blessed is the man [...] in whose spirit there is no guile.[1]

It is a tradition in the British Isles to sell sticks of candy rock at the seaside. Each stick has the name of the resort engraved through its middle. This advertising gimmick is a fascination to children, because, however much you suck the candy away—or wherever you break it—the name of the resort persists. The lettering is not just a veneer stuck on each end; it is an integral part of the candy.

Living the gospel should not be a veneer presented on the outside only. However I choose to divide my life or my being—work and home; public and private; family and friends; Sundays and weekdays; outer being and inner self[2]; words and deeds[3]; rules I apply to myself and rules I apply to others; belief and faith; motive and action[4]—I should find the name of Christ clearly apparent, a thread running through the whole of me.

Happiness is when what you think, what you say, and what you do are in harmony.[5]

Roman potters used to place a sign on their pots when they sold them, saying "sine cerum," meaning "without wax." It was a common trick to cover up cracks in pots by rubbing bees' wax into them. Of course, even the sign may have been a lie, so the untrusting customer would never purchase a pot that had not been standing in the sun for a while. From the practice of making and choosing pots genuinely "sine cerum" has come the word "sincere."

To attempt to deceive others by hiding by true motives or feelings—like rubbing wax in the cracks—shows a lack of integrity. In the scriptures, this is known as "guile." For instance, members of the select 144 thousand are described as being completely truthful—"in their mouth was found no guile"[6]—a quality listed along with chastity and perfection. Peter said of Jesus that he "did no sin, neither

Language of the Spirit

was guile found in his mouth: who, when he was reviled, reviled not again; when he suffered, he threatened not."[7]

To have integrity is to make every aspect of my life reflect the same set of gospel principles. It is to shun hypocrisy in its every manifestation. Jesus spent much of his time teaching against hypocrisy to those who lived the letter of the law but not the spirit, who had "a form of godliness but [denied] the power thereof,"[8] who would throw stones at others for sins they too had committed,[9] who judged others' motes while ignoring the beams in their own eyes.[10] I would do well to heed his teachings.

---

[1] Psalms 32: 2
[2] Luke 11: 39
[3] Isaiah 29: 13
[4] Moroni 7: 5-7
[5] Mahatma Gandhi (1869-1948), India spiritual leader and statesman
[6] Revelation 14: 4-5
[7] 1 Peter 2: 22-23
[8] 2 Timothy 3: 5
[9] John 8: 7
[10] Matthew 7: 3-5

33 Integrity

Three men walked down the road
As down the road walked he:
The man they saw,
The man he was,
And the man he hoped to be.[1]

It is inevitable that there are differences between how others see me and how I really am. The key to integrity though is to avoid deceit; not deliberately to project an image of myself to others to make them think that I am a person other than who I really am. The scriptures call this "guile"— the opposite of "frankness"—and "hypocrisy"—a form of dishonesty. Minimising the discrepancies between the "the man they [see]" and "the man [I am]" is one thing. Quite another is to recognise the differences between the man I am and the man I hope to be. Managing this difference is an important aspect of gospel living.

The key to focussing on "the man [I hope] to be" is to choose carefully my model. To what should I compare myself? The phrase "measure of creation" is used in some gospel contexts. Paul warns me that those "measuring themselves by themselves, and comparing themselves among themselves, are not wise."[2] My yardstick is the "measure of the stature of Christ."[3] The man I hope to be is more Christ-like than the man I am today. Living the gospel "shall greatly enlarge the soul without hypocrisy, and without guile."[4]

One of the qualities of those who inherit the celestial kingdom is that "they see as they are seen, and know as they are known."[5] This echoes the words of Paul: "now I know in part; but then I shall know even as also I am known."[6]

Reading the ancient accounts of Christ's life in the scriptures, and the words of Christ's living oracles, provide me with a daily reminder of the fourth man on that road of life: the man Christ wants me to be—the full measure of my creation, which is the model of Christ himself, which is the man I should hope to be.

Blessed is the man unto whom the Lord imputeth not iniquity, and in whose spirit there is no guile.[7]

---

[1] Unable to attribute this verse. First heard quoted in Sunday School, Solihull, England, by Brian Grant.
[2] 2 Corinthians 10: 12
[3] Ephesians 4: 13
[4] Doctrine and Covenants 121: 45
[5] Doctrine and Covenants 76: 94
[6] 1 Corinthians 13: 12
[7] Psalms 32: 2

34 Gratitude

In nothing doth man offend God, or against none is his wrath kindled, save those who confess not his hand in all things.[1]

When I was a missionary in Lyon, France, the front window of our apartment looked straight out onto a busy street. One morning, knowing I suppose that there were foreigners living there, two school boys knocked on the window and asked if we had any postage stamps. I had purposely been saving every English stamp that came on letter or parcel and I had quite a collection. So I was pleased to pass a few through the window.

The next morning there was another knock, and my companion and I were astonished to see ten or fifteen boys crowded round the window. "Timbres, timbres!" they demanded. I fetched my collection, and starting pressing a precious stamp into each upraised palm. But I was very quickly upset, for, without regard for the care with which I had collected them, or for the gift I was making, they snatched and crumpled the stamps and ran off without so much as a "merci."

On the following day, the knock on the window revealed a throng that had doubled again. This time though, they were to be disappointed. I made a little speech, explaining that unless they brought along their stamp collections and demonstrated that they were going to appreciate and care for the stamps, I would not give out any more.

Nobody came for over a week, and I was beginning to think I had been too harsh. Then, quite early one morning, there was a timid knock on our window. Two lads stood there with stamp albums under their arms. I invited them in, and spent a few minutes admiring their collections. Then I was pleased to present them with enough stamps to complete their English sets, knowing that they would be cared for and appreciated. They were delighted, and so was I, for the very purpose of my saving the stamps seemed to be fulfilled that day.

Language of the Spirit

Our Father in Heaven must feel toward me so much like I did with regard to those boys. He has so many blessings in store for me, and "delight[s] to honor those who serve [him]"[2] by opening the windows of heaven. But He is deeply saddened when I fail to appreciate how precious they are, or even where they came from.

It has been said that "gratitude is the most exquisite form of courtesy."[3] I would add that gratitude is the most explicit form of worship. It gladdens the spirit, it focuses the mind on God, the source of all our blessings, and it brings humility as I "confess His hand in all things."

---

[1] Doctrine and Covenants 59: 21

[2] Doctrine and Covenants 76: 5

[3] Jacques Maritain, French philosopher (1882-1973), *Reflections on America*, 1958

35 Beauty

> *Beauty is not in the face; beauty is a light in the heart [...]*
>
> *It is not the image you would see nor the song you would hear, But rather an image you see though you close your eyes and a song you hear though you shut your ears.*[1]

A recent discussion on BBC radio considered how blind people perceive beauty. Being fully-sighted, my sense of beauty is too much centred on sight. Blind me, and I would be too focussed on what I hear. And yet the blind and the deaf still have a sense of beauty.

One blind person described how travelling on the subway was an experience full of beauty; how the walkways and escalators guided her steps; how the wind on her face and the sound of the rails signalled the approach of the train; how the doors automatically opened for her; how the carriages magically transported her to another place. Yet my experience is limited to seeing the graffiti on the carriages, smelling the litter in the tunnel, and feeling the crush of the crowd. Does my sense of beauty not penetrate the surface of things?

Seeing only surface beauty goes hand-in-hand with hypocrisy. Where others strive to "appear beautiful outward, but are within full of [...] all uncleanness,"[2] the hypocrite in me refuses to see the unseemliness beyond obvious beauty, and fails to recognise true beauty beyond apparent unseemliness.

> *People are like stained glass windows—their true beauty can be seen only when there is light from within. The darker the night, the brighter the windows.*[3]

Actually, I prefer to view stained glass windows from within the cathedral, where their beauty is illuminated by the greater Light from without. The brighter the day, the greater the beauty within.

Language of the Spirit

The scriptures relate beauty to righteousness: "worship the Lord in the beauty of holiness."[4] David sings of dwelling, beholding, and enquiring in the temple. Balanced worship includes beholding beauty:

One thing have I desired of the Lord, that I will seek after; that I may dwell in the house of the Lord all the days of my life, to behold the beauty of the Lord, and to enquire in his temple.[5]

True beauty does not inspire profane or vulgar sentiments, such as fear or lust; only awe and wonder, a sense of the grace of God. My sense of beauty is God-given, and comes from my being created in His image.

---

[1] Kahlil Gibran
[2] Matthew 23: 27
[3] Elizabeth Kubler-Ross
[4] 1 Chronicles 16: 29
[5] Psalms 27: 4, emphasis added

36 Steadfastness

Lehi was desperately concerned for the plight of his wayward sons, Laman and Lemuel. His grief comes across in so many ways in his writings. For instance, as they were traveling in the wilderness, Lehi goes to the extent of naming a river and a valley after the two, and utters this lament:

> O that thou mightest be like this river, continually flowing into the fountain of all righteousness! [...] O that thou mightest be like unto this valley, firm and steadfast, and immovable in keeping the commandments of the Lord![1]

I find the following vocabulary used in the scriptures to describe steadfastness:

- *Firm*

    "Look to God with firmness of mind"[2]

    Moroni was "firm in the faith of Christ"[3]

    The Stripling Warriors' "minds were firm"[4]

    "Firmer and firmer in the faith"[5]

    "A firm mind in every form of godliness"[6]

    "Firm hope that ye shall one day rest"[7]

    "Firm in the hope of a glorious resurrection"[8]

- *Steadfast/fast*

    "Standing steadfastly in the faith"[9]

    "Be steadfast and immovable"[10]

    The Lamanites "do not stand fast in the faith of Christ"[11]

    "Hope [...] maketh an anchor [...] sure and steadfast"[12]

    "Stand fast in the work wherewith I have called you"[13]

    "He that remaineth steadfast [...] shall be saved"[14]

- *Strict*

    "Be strict in the plain road"[15]

- *Immovable*

    "Be steadfast and immovable"[16]

To continue Lehi's nature theme, Isaiah wishes that we "might be called trees of righteousness, the planting of the Lord,"[17] trees strong, firm, and immovable. I recently stood in a Redwood grove in Pfeiffer State Park, California. Those are big trees, so resistant to fire, disease, and storms that some of them live for 2000 years—the very embodiment of steadfastness.

---

[1] 1 Nephi 2: 9-10
[2] Jacob 3: 1-2
[3] Alma 48: 13
[4] Alma 57: 27
[5] Heleman 3: 35
[6] Moroni 7: 30
[7] Alma 34: 41
[8] Doctrine and Covenants 138: 14
[9] Mosiah 4: 11
[10] Mosiah 5: 15
[11] Alma 47: 27
[12] Isaiah 61: 3
[13] Ether 12: 4
[14] Doctrine and Covenants 9: 14
[15] Joseph Smith—Matthew 1: 11
[16] 2 Nephi 4: 32
[17] Mosiah 5: 15

37 Righteousness

Seek ye first the kingdom of God, and his righteousness.[1]

My first ever home teaching companion was Walter Stroebeck, a German national. We were students together in London. We had fourteen families on our list, and we used to go out twice a week. He drove his left-hand drive Volkswagen Beetle, and I navigated through the labyrinth of West London streets. This was when I first encountered the ambiguity of the English language for giving directions. The problem centres on the word "right." I found myself using it in five ways: first, to indicate a right turn; second, to mean "all the way," as in "Right to the end"; third, as a an interjection, "Right, now turn left!"; fourthly, to indicate timeliness, as in "Turn left right now!"; and fifthly, as an indication of correctness "Go that way! That's right." Ample confusion if English is not your first language! We did laugh about it.

My dictionary actually has 51 distinct uses for the word "right," and that's not counting the nuances within those meanings. Fascinating is the connection between "left" and "right" and "right" and "wrong." "Christ sitteth on the right hand of God,"[2] and at the Day of Judgement, the Lord will separate the just from the unjust, "and he shall set the sheep on his right hand, but the goats on the left."[3] It seems that the *right*eous are those who will sit on the *right* hand of God.

It is not only in the English language that this connection exists. In French, the words "la gauche" and "la droit" mean left and right, and "le droit" means "the law." In German, the word "recht" has the same double meaning. The righteous are those who live the law of God.

The simplest scriptural definition of "righteousness" is to be "right in the sight of God,"[4] in other words, to keep his commandments. This is echoed in the words of the Lord in relation to the "Shakers": "they are not right before me and must needs repent."[5]

Language of the Spirit

Righteousness is the key to surviving the great traumas that will visit the Earth prior to the Second Coming: "[God] will not suffer that the wicked shall destroy the righteous"; "he will preserve the righteous by his power"; "wherefore the righteous need not fear"; "the righteous shall not perish"; and "because of the righteousness of his people, Satan has no power."[6]

Abraham named himself as a "follower of righteousness" and sought to be a "greater follower of righteousness" by seeking "the *right* where unto [he] should be ordained to administer" in the priesthood. Through the priesthood, "[he] became a *rightful* heir, a High Priest, holding the *right* belonging to the fathers."[7]

---

[1] Matthew 6: 33

[2] Colossians 3: 1 (See also Acts 7: 55)

[3] Matthew 25: 33 (See also verses 34 and 41)

[4] Acts 8: 21

[5] Doctrine and Covenants 49: 2

[6] 1 Nephi 22: 16-26

[7] Abraham 1: 2, emphasis added

38 Persecution

> *Blessed are they which are persecuted for righteousness' sake: for theirs is the kingdom of heaven. Blessed are ye, when men shall revile you, and persecute you, and say all manner of evil against you falsely, for my sake. Rejoice and be exceedingly glad: [...] for so persecuted they the prophets which were before you.*[1]

Expect persecution, but never persecute. Persecution is a form of hatred, and is always motivated by pride. It is usually those in an obvious position of power that bully the seemingly powerless: the rich despise the poor instead of sharing their plenty;[2] the worldly-"wise" mock the saintly-"ignorant" instead of hearing the truth.[3] You can seldom change someone through persecution, for persecution almost always reinforces the persecutable behaviour.

Persecution takes many forms: mocking, bullying, ridicule, belittlement, segregation, denial of rights, torture or killing. Jesus suffered them all. True followers of Jesus can expect to experience some, for "all that will live godly in Christ Jesus shall suffer persecution."[4] I should react to my persecutors with the opposite of hatred. Here is a scriptural checklist:

> Love them. (Matthew 5: 44)
> Pray for them. (Acts 7: 60; 3 Nephi 12: 44)
> Bless them. (Romans 12: 14)
>
> Proclaim the gospel to them. (Doctrine and Covenants 99: 1) Rejoice in being "worthy to suffer shame for his name." (Acts 5: 41; 3 Nephi 12: 10; Matthew 10: 22; Doctrine and Covenants 101: 35)
>
> Wax stronger. (Doctrine and Covenants 122: 7; Heleman 3: 34–35)

Remember, that to persecute Jesus' followers is to persecute Him;[5] and that to persecute Jesus is to persecute His followers.[6]

Finally, persecution cannot separate us from the love of Christ;[7] it can only bring us closer.

Persecuted, but not forsaken.[8]

---

[1] Matthew 5: 10-12
[2] 2 Nephi 9: 30
[3] Heleman 3: 33-36; 1 Nephi 8: 26-27
[4] 2 Timothy 3: 12
[5] Acts 9: 4
[6] John 15: 20
[7] Romans 8: 35
[8] 2 Corinthians 4: 9

39 Pride

Pride is the universal sin, the great vice.[1]

In the general conference of the church in April 1989, President Ezra Taft Benson gave a talk that impressed me so much that I marked every one of the 107 references he used as a long chain in my scriptures. His theme was pride, which he portrays as the universal sin. In contrast to *love*—the principle by which our Father in Heaven rules over us, and on which hang all His commandments[2]—"the central feature of pride is enmity—enmity toward God and enmity toward our fellow men. Enmity means 'hatred toward, hostility to, or a state of opposition.' It is the power by which Satan wishes to reign over us."[1]

The following are further quotes from his sermon:

"Pride is essentially competitive in nature." "Pride is ugly. It says, 'If you succeed, I am a failure.'" In the words of C. S. Lewis:

> *Pride gets no pleasure out of having something, only out of having more of it than the next man. [...] It is the comparison that makes you proud: the pleasure of being above the rest. Once the element of competition has gone, pride has gone.[3]*

"It was through pride that Lucifer fell. It was through pride that Christ was crucified. It was through pride that Saul became an enemy to David. It was through pride that King Noah burned Abinadi.

"Pride is a sin that can readily be seen in others but is rarely admitted in ourselves. Most of us consider pride to be a sin of those on the top, such as the rich and the learned, looking down at the rest of us.[4] There is, however, a far more common ailment among us—and that is pride from the bottom looking up. It is manifest in so many ways, such as faultfinding, gossiping, backbiting, murmuring, living beyond our means, envying, coveting, withholding gratitude and praise that might lift another, and being unforgiving and jealous."

Language of the Spirit

"The antidote for pride is humility—meekness, submissiveness.[5] It is the broken heart and contrite spirit.[6]" "We can choose to humble ourselves by conquering enmity toward our brothers and sisters, esteeming them as ourselves, and lifting them as high as or higher than we are."[7]

"Let us choose to be humble. We can do it. I know we can."

---

[1] President Ezra Taft Benson, "Beware of Pride", *Ensign*, May 1989

[2] Matthew 22: 40

[3] Clive Staples Lewis, English author (1898-1963), *Mere Christianity*, New York: Macmillan, 1952, pp. 109-10.

[4] See 2 Nephi 9: 42

[5] See Alma 7: 23

[6] See 3 Nephi 9: 20; 3 Nephi 12: 19; Doctrine and Covenants 20: 37; 59: 8; Psalms 34: 18; Isaiah 57: 15; Isaiah 66: 2

[7] See Doctrine and Covenants 38: 24; 81: 5; 84: 106

40 Indifference

The opposite of love is not hate, it's indifference.
The opposite of art is not ugliness, it's indifference.
The opposite of faith is not heresy, it's indifference.
And the opposite of life is not death, it's indifference.[1]

Ignorance is indifference to learning.
Sloth is indifference to industry.
Weakness is indifference to strength.[2]

Opposites are often not so opposite. I remember someone pointing out that expressions of joy and fear on the human face are similar in many ways. In both cases the eyes are wide and the mouth is drawn back to show the teeth, either in delight or in panic.

Since love and hate are both passionate, they share indifference as an opposite. "Passionate indifference" is an oxymoron. Like most people, I exhibit the apathy of indifference far more often than I experience the passion of hate. For all practical purposes, therefore, I should consider indifference to be the opposite of love.

> *When one is indifferent, the spirit remains apathetic and detached. There is then a natural lack of any involvement that would lead to faith. Certainly no man can be saved in indifference.*[3]

Faith is belief that motivates me to action; indifference lulls me into inaction. One of Satan's strategies is to "pacify, and lull [...] into carnal security."[4] In contrast, the prophet cries: "arouse the faculties of your souls; shake yourselves that ye may awake from the slumber of death!"[5]

> *Washing one's hands of the conflict between the powerful and the powerless means to side with the powerful, not to be neutral.*[6]

Language of the Spirit

To be indifferent is not to be neutral. To the Laodiceans, the Lord said, "I know thy works, that art neither cold nor hot; I would thou wert cold or hot. So then because thou art lukewarm, and neither cold nor hot, I will spue thee out of my mouth."[7] To be indifferent is usually to side with evil, which thrives on inaction. Be it not said of me that I "passed by on the other side,"[8] or that I asked "Am I my brother's keeper?"[9]

To choose indifference is to choose to exist without really living. I was not indifferent when I chose mortality for its love and hate, beauty and ugliness, faith and heresy, life and death. I was passionate. I "shouted for joy."[10]

---

[1] Eliezer Wiesel, Romanian author, holocaust survivor (1928-)
[2] Sterling W. Sill, *The Three I's*, New Era, Aug. 1979, 4
[3] Ibid.
[4] 2 Nephi 28: 21
[5] Jacob 3: 11
[6] Paulo Freire, Brazilian educationalist (1921 - 1997)
[7] Revelation 3: 15-16
[8] Luke 10: 31
[9] Genesis 4: 9
[10] Job 38: 7

41 Selfishness

Qu'est-ce qu'un égoiste ?
C'est quelqu'un qui ne s'intéresse à moi !

I found this saying printed on the back of a sweet wrapper in France: "What is an egoist? Someone who is not interested in me!"

Charles Dickens placed the following words in the mouth of his character Martin Chuzzlewit:

> *There is a kind of selfishness—I have learned it of my own experience of my own breast—which is constantly on the watch for selfishness in others; and in holding others at a distance by suspicions and distrusts, wonders why they don't approach, and don't confide, and call this selfishness in others.*[1]

I have determined never to accuse another of being selfish, most especially when the apparent selfishness is directed against me. For the cry, or even the thought, "you are *so* selfish!" is itself a manifestation of selfishness.

The scriptures don't seem to talk explicitly about selfishness. But many of Jesus' teachings are about replacing self-centredness with service to others. Look, for instance, at this commentary on the Parable of the Good Samaritan:

> *The lawyer asks 'Who is my neighbour?' At the end Jesus poses a different question: 'Which of these three proved neighbour to the man who fell among robbers?' The lawyer's question puts himself at the centre. Who is his neighbour? But the parable transforms the question: it is the wounded man who is the centre now. Who was neighbour to him?*[2]

Self-centredness runs deep in the veins of the natural man. It is manifest here in a young man's seemingly innocent question, which Jesus turns right round to focus on the other person. The Lord invites

Language of the Spirit

me to *be* a neighbour, not just to have one. The Lord would draw me out of myself. He would have me define myself—and my life—in terms of how I can be of service to others.

---

[1] Charles Dickens (1812-1870), English author, *"Martin Chuzzlewit"*, Chapter 52

[2] Timothy Radcliffe (1945-), General Master of the Order of Preachers (Dominican), *The Parable of the Good Samaritan*, lecture given in Camaldoli, 30 June 2001, www.op.org/international/english/Documents/ masters_order/ Radcliffe/samaritan.htm

42 Greed

When I was about ten years old, my father taught me a subtle lesson. It was nearly Christmas, and it was a tradition for the men of the family to go shopping for gifts for Mummy. The town was very busy, and in the press of paying for some purchases, I noticed that my father had received the wrong change. When I pointed this out, he stopped to count the coins, and then said something like this: "Well if she had given me too much change, I would have gone back to the shop; but seeing as I am the one who is short, then let's not worry about it."

Now to a ten-year-old, that was a very interesting attitude. It was precisely the opposite of my sentiments at the time. If I had been short-changed, I would definitely have gone back; if I had been given too much change, I would have rejoiced in the good fortune! By being concerned about the shop assistant being short at the end of the day, my father was showing compassion for another. In contrast, I was merely being greedy, that self-centred attribute of wanting to accumulate money or possessions at someone else's expense.

Theft is more often motivated by naked greed that it is by genuine need. Any person faced with the choice of stealing or starving deserves some sympathy. But the Lord makes a distinction in the attitudes of the poor:

> *Wo unto you poor men [...] whose hands are not stayed from laying hold upon other men's goods, whose eyes are full of greediness [...] !*
>
> *But blessed are the poor who are pure in heart [...] for the fatness of the earth shall be theirs.*[1]

Attitude is everything. Indeed, just the inner sentiment of greed is a form of theft, even if no actual theft results. The attitude that displaces

Language of the Spirit

greed is perhaps generosity, and the commandment "thou shalt not steal"[2] could have its corollary in "generous shalt thou be."

Recently my wife showed me another example of what an attitude of generosity means. When selling our house, we received an offer that was twenty thousand pounds below the asking price. My reaction was, "No way! Think what we could do with all that money!" My wife said, "Let's not be greedy. We may wait months for the asking price." We sold at the amount offered, and have not suffered in the slightest from the financial shortfall. In fact, an attitude of generosity eased the contractual exchanges, encouraged friendships, and made for a pleasant experience.

And so it is only years later that I am learning to appreciate the lesson on greed and generosity my father taught that day. God's grace is an act of generosity; if I am to be like Christ, there is no place for greed. Generous shall I be.

---

[1] Doctrine and Covenants 56: 16-17
[2] Exodus 20: 15

43 Life and Murder

Ye have heard that it was said [to][1] them of old time, Thou shalt not kill;[2] and whosoever shall kill shall be in danger of the judgment: But I say unto you,

- *That whosoever is angry with his brother without a cause shall be in danger of the judgment:*
- *And whosoever shall say to his brother, Raca, shall be in danger of the council;*
- *But whosoever shall say, Thou fool, shall be in danger of hell fire.*[3]

Murder is not an everyday temptation for most of us; the sixth commandment may seem an easy one to keep. But in his Sermon on the Mount, Jesus reviews this commandment in terms of the inward motivation rather the outward act. In doing this, he shows how even this commandment actually touches our everyday lives.

The structure of what Jesus says is interesting. For emphasis, he essentially repeats the same thing three times: anger and judgment, Raca and the council,[4] "Thou fool" and hell. "Raca" is thought to be related to an Aramaic word meaning "empty," and is used here as a derisive term, indicating worthlessness. So Jesus' choice of terms seems to cover anger, derision, scorn, disdain, mockery, ridicule, contempt, and disrespect.

When I allow myself to entertain such sentiments, who knows where it will lead? Perhaps not as far as murder; but thoughts that are derisive to others are nonetheless the seeds of murder. To think these thoughts is harmful as much to myself as to others. It shrinks rather than promotes my ability, and that of others, to live a full life.

[1] The Greek reads "to" rather than "by."

[2] Exodus 20: 13

[3] Matthew 5: 21-22, emphasis added. It is interesting that the phrase "without cause" is translated from a Greek word meaning "lightly," which is absent in the earliest manuscripts.

[4] Referring to the Jewish supreme court, the Sanhedrin.

44 Vulgarity and Profanity

Ye are a chosen generation, a royal priesthood, an holy nation, a peculiar people.[1]

As a youngster, I used thoroughly to enjoy listening to the BBC Radio 4 comedy programmes. The whole family would turn on the wireless at six-thirty in the evening, and laugh together at "The Goon Show," "The Navy Lark," or Kenneth Horne's "Round the Horn." However, I cannot listen to today's equivalent. The shows are so full of completely unacceptable language that I no longer turn on the radio for the comedy hour.

I am increasingly conscious of the widening gap between what is acceptable in the street and the Gospel standards I choose to live. Peter called the saints—the followers of Christ—"a peculiar people" in the sense of belonging to the Lord; but in the modern sense of the word, we are an ever more "peculiar people" when compared to the surrounding society. And yet it is the world that changes, not the Lord's definition of righteousness.

The use of vulgar and profane language is one very obvious differentiator. The Latin origins of the two terms "vulgar" and "profane" have a story to tell. "Vulgar" comes from "vulgus" meaning "the common people," or "the crowd"—the very opposite of "peculiar." If I use vulgar language, I fail to make myself different from those around me. I am not one of God's "peculiar people."

"Profane" comes from "pro-," meaning "outside," and "fanus," meaning "temple." The term "profanus" was used to refer to people who were forbidden from entering temples. If I use profane language, I am using language that would be unacceptable inside the temple. I may even disqualify myself from entering the temple.

If vulgar and profane language is merely "colourful," as many would have us believe, then I am unashamedly "colour-prejudice" when

Language of the Spirit

it comes to certain words. I try to remember that white is worn in the temple, not just as a symbol of purity, but of the universality of the love and mercy of Jesus Christ. White is, after all, the full and balanced combination of all colours of the spectrum.

> *Christ in the heart of every man who thinks of me,*
> *Christ in the mouth of every man who speaks of me,*
> *Christ in the eye that sees me,*
> *Christ in the ear that hears me.*[2]

If I am to serve God with my mouth, I will choose clean, uplifting, merciful, loving language. The colour of my words will be temple white.

---

[1] 1 Peter 2: 9
[2] Attributed to Patrick, the patron saint of Ireland, Circa 377 AD

45 Idolatry

> *Surely your turning of things upside down shall be esteemed as the potter's clay: for shall the work say of him that made it, He made me not? Or shall the thing framed say of him that framed it, He had no understanding?*[1]

Those who serve mammon[2] rather than God have turned things upside down. Man claims to have created God rather than God having created man; they worship things created rather than worshipping the Creator; they bow down to the things they have themselves created rather than to Him who has created them. Such warped worship is clearly identified by Paul as idolatry: they "worshipped and served the creature rather than the creator."[3]

In the introductory section of the Doctrine and Covenants, the Lord explains that:

> *The inhabitants of the earth [...] seek not the Lord to establish his righteousness, but every man walketh in his own way, and after the image of his own god, whose image is in the likeness of the world, and whose substance is that of an idol.*[4]

There is no doubt that man can create beautiful things, worthy of admiration. The world is terribly taken with technology. Every time I admire a sleek motor car, or the latest design of mobile phone, I am treading on the borders of idolatry. And Paul is careful to remind me that covetousness is a form of idolatry.[5]

The world is also terribly taken with people. Acres of paper and pixels are devoted to portraying, displaying, and gossiping about people. Colourful pages make sportsmen, actors, politicians and singers into heroes, and invite me to admire, imitate, and worship them.

Rather, I should keep things the right way up by worshiping the Creator rather than man's creations. I should keep the first two of the Ten Commandments.

> *Thou shalt have no other gods before me. Thou shalt not make unto thee any graven image, or any likeness of any thing that is in heaven above, or that is in the earth beneath, or that is in the water under the earth: Thou shalt not bow thyself down to them, nor serve them.*[6]

I should know my place, and with Isaiah declare:

> *But now, O Lord, thou art our father; we are the clay, and thou our potter; and we all are the work of thy hand.*[7]

---

[1] Isaiah 29: 16

[2] Luke 16: 13

[3] Romans 1: 25. ("Creature" can be translated as "creation.")

[4] Doctrine and Covenants 1: 16

[5] Colossians 3: 5

[6] Exodus 20: 3-5

[7] Isaiah 64: 8

Language of the Spirit

46 Materialism

When you look at others with their lands and gold,
Think that Christ has promised you his wealth untold.
Count your many blessings; money cannot buy
Your reward in heaven nor your home on high.[1]

Materialism tends to focus on the here-and-now, on instant pleasure and gratification, and is blind to the future: "eat and drink and be merry, for tomorrow we die."[2] It is a buy-now-pay-later culture—sacrificing the future for the present.

Looking to the future, of course, requires faith. But however forward looking, faith does not sacrifice the present for the future; it allows me to live the present to the full; it brokers a balance. Living faithfully brings me "peace in this world, *and* eternal life in the world to come."[3] Even though gospel principles eschew immediate pleasure in favour of things I can do now to obtain a fullness of joy later, living them still brings me immediate peace. Thus righteous living leaves no feeling of being hard-done-by; it is an entirely positive thing.

Only faithful living brings the reward of eternal life. Just as money cannot buy the rewards of heaven, neither can it buy the "peace in this world" that the faithful are promised. Lands and gold bring trouble, envy, and anxiety far more often than peace.

Present peace and future joy are connected. The "peace in this world" is the reassurance of the Spirit that I am on the right path. It is my "assurance of things hoped for, the evidence of things not seen."[4] Paul refers several times to this principle. Sometimes he refers to it in terms of "the firstfruits of the Spirit [that I might] with patience wait for"[5] the later fruits. Elsewhere he says "ye were sealed with that holy Spirit of promise, which is the earnest of our inheritance until the redemption of the purchased possession."[6] The expression "earnest of our inheritance" is in the obsolete sense of a promissory payment

Language of the Spirit

in advance of full payment. The "purchased possession" is the place that the Saviour has bought for me through the Atonement. As He promised His disciples, "I go to prepare a place for you."[7]

So righteous living both requires faith and fosters faith; it gives me reassurance now that I might "with surety hope for a better world"[8] to come. It helps me to escape the mill-stone that would anchor me to the material world.

---

[1] Johnson Oatman Jr., "Count your Blessings," *Hymns of the Church of Jesus Christ of Latter-Day Saints*, No. 1, verse 3

[2] 2 Nephi 28: 7, quoting Isaiah 22: 13.

[3] Doctrine and Covenants 59: 23, emphasis added

[4] Hebrews 11: 1

[5] Romans 8: 23, 25

[6] Ephesians 1: 14. See also 2 Corinthians 1: 22; 5: 5

[7] John 14: 2

[8] Ether 12: 4

47 Possessions

Where your treasure is, there will be your heart also.[1]

In August 1997, Diana Princess of Wales died in Paris in an accident that shook the world. That event and the noise of its aftermath eclipsed the death of another great person: Mother Teresa of Calcutta. The contrast between some aspects of the two lives and deaths are stark. Diana, already from a wealthy family herself, married into the Royal Family, with all that that implies. In comparison, Mother Teresa's vow of poverty, which served her so well in working with the poor, meant that her only possessions when she died were her habit, her sandals and the pail in which she washed. She did not need material possessions to make a material difference.

The accoutrements of a particular way of life are sometimes called "trappings." It is true that material possessions are a form of bondage. The old saying, "I never have to worry about money, because I just don't have any!" is accurate. With wealth comes worry. Material possessions tie me to material values.

Jesus was able to go straight to the central issue of each individual's heart. A particular young man's worldly possessions caused him to walk away from Christ rather than follow Him:

> *Jesus said unto him, If thou wilt be perfect, go and sell all that thou hast, and give to the poor, and thou shalt have treasure in heaven: and come follow me. But when the young man heard that saying, he went away sorrowful: for he had great possessions.[2]*

Possessions are all right as long as my heart is not set upon them.

My wife, Yvonne, does not accumulate possessions for the sake of it, but disposes easily of things that have become non-essential. In contrast, I have great difficulty throwing things away. I have been

Language of the Spirit

known to search through the recycling bins to check for things that may have been discarded without my knowledge. If I do recover anything, it is invariably something that is very surprised to see me, for I will not have touched it for years. Little by little, Yvonne is teaching me to release my heart from material trappings, and turn its affections to more lasting treasures.

The gospel educates my desires, and teaches me to say, "I have sufficient for my needs."

---

[1] Matthew 6: 21
[2] Matthew 19: 21-22

48 The Golden Rule

All things whatsoever ye would that men should do to you, do ye even so to them: for this is the law and the prophets.[1]

The Golden Rule—sometimes called the "ethic of reciprocity"—is found in the scriptures of most religions, as attested by the examples given below. It appears in the Gospels in many forms, the most direct being the citation above. As hinted by Jesus in this passage, it is often regarded as the most concise and general principle of ethics.

Judaism: "What is hateful to you, do not do to your neighbour: that is the whole Torah; all the rest of it is commentary; go and learn."[2]

Islam: "No one of you is a believer until he desires for his brother that which he desires for himself."[3]

Hinduism: "One should not behave towards others in a way which is disagreeable to oneself. This is the essence of morality. All other activities are due to selfish desire."[4]

Buddhism: "Hurt not others with that which pains yourself."[5]

Confucianism: "Tsekung asked, Is there one word that can serve as a principle of conduct for life? Confucius replied, It is the word *shu*—reciprocity: Do not do to others what you do not want them to do to you."[6]

Bahá'í: "And if thine eyes be turned towards justice, choose thou for thy neighbour that which thou choosest for thyself."[7]

Zoroastrianism: "Whatever is disagreeable to yourself do not do unto others."[8]

Greek philosophy: "Do not do unto others what angers you if done to you by others."[9]

Jainism: "A man should wander about treating all creatures as he himself would be treated."[10]

African Tradition: "One going to take a pointed stick to pinch a baby bird should first try it on himself to feel how it hurts."[11]

---

[1] Matthew 7: 12
[2] Talmud, Shabbat 31a
[3] Forty Hadith of an-Nawawi 13
[4] Mahabharata, Anusasana Parva 113: 8
[5] Udana-Varga
[6] Analects 15: 23-24
[7] Epistle to the Son of the Wolf 30
[8] Shayast-na-Shayast 13: 29
[9] Isocrates (436-338 BCE)
[10] Sutrakritanga 1.11.33
[11] Yoruba Proverb (Nigeria)

Language of the Spirit

49 Ethic of Pure Love

As I have loved you [...] love one another.[1]

Contrast the Ethic of Reciprocity—"do unto others as you would have them do unto you"[2]—with the Law of Retribution: "life for life, eye for eye, tooth for tooth, hand for hand, foot for foot."[3] This law could almost be framed as an "Ethic of Retaliation"—"do unto others as they have done unto you." Another expression of this ethic is "do unto him as he had thought to have done unto his brother,"[4] expressed in the context of those who bear false witness. As is clear from the Sermon on Mount this ethic was believed amongst the Jews in Jesus' time:

> *You have heard it hath been said, Thou shalt love thy neighbour, and hate thine enemy. But I say unto you, Love your enemies, bless them that curse you, do good to them that hate you.*[5]

Retaliation and reciprocity are different in nature. Firstly, retaliation describes how to react to another; in contrast, reciprocity describes the initiation of action based on the imagined actions of others. Secondly, retaliation propagates actions, whether good or evil, whereas reciprocity is capable of cutting off the propagation of evil for evil, and replacing it with good.

Retaliation is a characteristic of the "natural man,"[6] which I strive to avoid, for "evil multiplies by the response it seeks to provoke. [...] The chain of evil is broken for good when a pure and loving heart absorbs a hurt and forbears to hurt in return."[7] I can constantly cut off the propagation of evil and bad feeling, by living the highest form of reciprocity: "love thy neighbour as thyself"[8] and "as I have loved you [...] love one another."[9]

Notice that this last commandment overcomes an inherent weakness in the Golden Rule, which makes no statement about how I should want to be treated by others. I may have low expectations or perverted

Language of the Spirit

views of how I should be treated, and thus apply the Golden Rule by treating others in an inappropriate way. By using Jesus as my model of love, however, I know how I should treat others; not necessarily in the way they treat me (retaliation), nor according to the poor image I have of myself (reciprocity), but simply in the way that Jesus loves me.

So Jesus, as always, exposes me to higher values, replacing retaliation—however just it may seem—and reciprocity—however right it may seem—with something higher than both: the ethic of pure love.

---

[1] John 13: 34

[2] See Matthew 7: 12

[3] Exodus 21: 22-25

[4] See Matthew 7: 12

[5] Matthew 5: 43-44

[6] Mosiah 3: 19

[7] Dennis Rasmussen, LDS philosopher, *The Lord's Question,* 2nd Edition, BYU Press, Provo, 2001, p. 66

[8] Matthew 22: 37. See also Mosiah 27: 4.

[9] John 13: 34

50 Law of Restoration

> *Man receives only that which he gives. The Game of Life is a game of boomerangs. Man's thoughts, deeds and words, return to him sooner or later, with astounding accuracy. This is the law of Karma, which is Sanskrit for "Comeback."*[1]
>
> *There is a destiny that makes us brothers;*
>   *None goes his way alone:*
> *All that we send into the lives of others*
>   *Comes back into our own.*[2]
>
> *That which ye do send out shall return unto you again, and be restored; therefore, the word restoration more fully condemneth the sinner, and justifieth him not at all.*[3]
>
> *Ye can do good and [...] have that which is good restored unto you; or ye can do evil, and have that which is evil restored unto you.*[4]

Whatever I send out to others—in the form of words, feelings, signals or messages—the same will eventually be returned to me, for good or for bad. If this restoration does not occur in this life, then I can be certain that it will in the next.

It seems that the principle of "Karma"—called by Alma the "Law of Restoration" [3]—is both a natural law and a law of heavenly justice. A natural law is one which describes the nature of the universe, and which cannot be broken—like the law of gravity. "And that's the way it is."[5] Rules of law, however, may be set up by God or man to predicate consequences upon actions. They require judgement to be applied.

If I am consistently generous and gracious to others, others will be generous and gracious to me. This is the natural part of the Law of Restoration. Even the natural man tends to return good for good. (It takes, perhaps, the spiritual man to return good for evil.)[6]

In addition, God's law stipulates that if I judge unrighteously, for instance, I will be similarly judged, probably by God himself at that "great and dreadful day"[7]—great for the repentant, dreadful for the unrepentant.

> *Judge not unrighteously, that ye be not judged: but judge righteous judgement. For with what judgement ye judge, ye shall be judged: and with what measure ye mete, it shall be measured unto you again.*[8]

---

[1] Florence Scovel Shinn, Author (1871-1940), *The Game of Life (and How to Play It)*, Chapter 5

[2] "A Creed", Edwin Markham, American poet

[3] Alma 41: 15

[4] Heleman 13: 32

[5] Bishop H. David Burton, "And that's the way it is," *Ensign,* April 2003

[6] Matthew 5: 44 ; Romans 12: 14-21

[7] Malachi 4: 5

[8] Matthew 7: 2 (JST). See also Doctrine and Covenants 1: 10.

51 Extrapolation

Elder Boyd K. Packer, presiding once at the Reading England stake conference, taught the principle of extrapolation: *if you want an inkling of what the fruits of a particular idea will be, imagine its effect on society if every person in the world lived that idea.*

A negative example: on a hot day in the office, I go to the water cooler, pick up a plastic cup, drink from it, and throw the cup in the bin. Imagine the effect on society if every person in the world were to do that, even once a day: it would be an ecological disaster! Drinking fountains may be better.

A positive example: I like the idea of leaving the world a better place. It is a principle that can be applied in big ways—over the span of a life-time—or in small ways—from minute to minute. Every time I visit the kitchen, for instance, I try to find a way of leaving it slightly cleaner, slightly tidier, than when I entered. Now imagine the effect on society if every person followed this principle. The world would be spotless, and no cleaners would be required. (There may be a problem with people being too obsessive, though!)

The same imagination exercise reveals the futility of seeking revenge. Gandhi's extrapolation lead to this statement: "An eye for an eye will make the whole world blind."[1] In contrast, consider the virtues of returning good for evil: imagine society if every person were able to return good for evil in all situations. How long would evil last? Is that what will happen during the millennium, when Satan shall be bound[2] and "because of the righteous of [God's] people, [he] has no power"?[3]

> *Hatreds never cease by hatreds in this world. By love alone they cease. This is an ancient law.* [4]

In an editorial comment, Mormon makes an extrapolation relating to the character of Captain Moroni:

Language of the Spirit

If all men had been, and were, and ever would be, like unto Moroni, behold, the very powers of hell would have been shaken forever; yea, the devil would never have power over the hearts of the children of men.[5]

Jesus was Moroni's model, and mine. It is His image that I should strive to imitate, propagate, and extrapolate. There is not one thing that Jesus taught that, if universally applied by all of mankind, would not leave the world a vastly better place.

---

[1] Mahatma Gandhi (1869-1948), Indian spiritual leader and statesman

[2] Revelation 20: 2; Doctrine and Covenants 84: 100

[3] 1 Nephi 22: 26

[4] Dhammapada (5), Buddhist scripture

[5] Alma 48: 17

52 Reflexivity

The quality of mercy is not strain'd;
It droppeth as the gentle rain from heaven
Upon the place beneath. It is twice blessed:
It blesseth him that gives and him that takes.[1]

Shakespeare's description of mercy being "twice blessed" applies to many gospel virtues. A simple smile transmits kindness to another, and simultaneously transforms the giver's spiritual and physical well-being. An attitude of forgiveness heals the forgiver more than the forgiven. This is a kind of reflexivity, because the gift reflects back on the giver. Gospel giving is not like spending money. I cannot spend a smile. Sharing my testimony does not consume it, but invigorates it. Smiling and testimony are not finite resources; they are somehow self-generating. As philosopher Deepak Chopra puts is, "Anything that is of value in life only multiplies when it is given."[2]

The same is true of vices. To carry anger in my heart poisons my own soul more than the souls of those who are the subject of my anger. Hence this burning image:

The hatred you're carrying is a live coal in your heart—far more damaging to yourself than to them.[3]

Indeed, vices too have a tendency to multiply themselves. "Evil propagates itself by the reaction it seeks to provoke in others."[4] Just as it takes a conscious effort *not* to smile in response to a genuine smile, so it takes a conscious effort not to return evil for evil.

Knowing that my knowledge of the Spirit can only grow in the sharing, why am I so hesitant to speak of it? I know people who radiate goodness; who have the ability in turn to lift and illuminate those around them. Their positive feelings are infectious. Can I learn to be such a person?

Language of the Spirit

Life engenders life. Energy creates energy. It is by spending oneself that one becomes rich.[5]

Rather than fear diminishment in sharing, I should learn to deal out from "the barrel of meal [that] shall not waste," and "the cruse of oil [that shall not] fail."[6] When I render service, I do not "fling my soul-wealth away"[7]; it is an investment. I should not forget that in reality such sharing twice blesses, that is, it blesses both the giver and taker.

The fragrance always remains in the hand that gives the rose.[8]

---

[1] William Shakespeare, *The Merchant of Venice,* Act 4, Scene 1, 179-192 (Alexander Text)

[2] Deepak Chopra, American doctor

[3] Lawana Blackwell, Author, *The Dowry of Miss Lydia Clark, 1999*

[4] *The Lord's Question,* Dennis Rasmussen, 2nd Edition, BYU Press, Provo, 2001, p. 66

[5] Sarah Bernhardt, French actress (1844-1923), real name Rosine Nernard

[6] 1 Kings 17: 14

[7] "Rock to me to sleep", Elizabeth Akers Allen, poet

[8] Hada Bejar, Actress, quoted in *Peacemaking: Day by Day,* vol. 2, p. 54, pub. Pax Christi (1989)

53 Luck

When I told a friend[1] of a blessing I had recently received, she said, "That was lucky!" Whilst appreciating the sentiment, I could not help thinking that it was not "luck" at all, so I suggested to her that we should find an acronym for the word "luck" that somehow related it to gospel blessings. To my astonishment, she came out almost immediately with the suggestion: "Living Under Christ's Kindness"—a masterpiece!

I once heard President Thomas S. Monson say that "very few things happen by chance."[2] I contemplated this thought as I nursed a fractured ankle. An "unlucky" accident that took a few seconds to occur promised months of disruption and inconvenience to self, family, and employer. However, I remain convinced that it was supposed to happen. If I am prepared to accept the "lucky" in life, then I must also allow the "unlucky."

Just because things were "supposed to happen" does not mean that they are always caused by God. Although He undoubtedly has the power to do so, He does not constantly micro-manage the affairs of this world. I believe the vicissitudes of life lead to events that God *permits* to occur, in that He chooses not to prevent them. But whether caused or permitted, it is incumbent upon me to seek out the underlying meaning of my blessings and afflictions.

The priesthood administration I requested over my broken ankle blessed me to find the reason. I used some of the space created in my life by the incident to engage in serious reflection.

The test of this probationary life is "to see if they will do all things whatsoever the Lord their God shall command them."[3] All "lucky" or "unlucky" events in my life are all part of the same test.

I like something that Dennis E. Simmons, a member of the First Quorum of Seventy, said at conference:

Language of the Spirit

He has the power, but it's our test.

What does the Lord expect of us with respect to our challenges? He expects us to do all we can do. He does the rest. Nephi said, "For we know that it is by grace that we are saved, after all we can do."[4,5]

So now, whenever I hear the word "luck," I think immediately of the grace of Jesus Christ. Even when I am "unlucky," I should remember that grace. So maybe "unlucky" means "UNconditionally Living Under Christ's Kindness."

---

[1] Marilyn Saunders, Newbury Branch, Reading England Stake, 2004

[2] President Thomas S. Monson, UK Regional Priesthood Leadership, 29 April 2000

[3] Abraham 3: 25

[4] 2 Nephi 25: 23

[5] "But if not…", *Ensign*, May 2004, p. 75

54 Potential

*Now we are the sons of God,
and it doth not yet appear what we shall be:
but we know that [...] we shall be like him.*[1]

"FREE Wheel of Destiny: love, luck, health and wealth—use it and discover your potential!" announces a contemporary women's magazine.[2] I am invited to stick a pin into a chart of numbers, and look up a corresponding sentence. "This oracle can be used both to answer specific questions and give you a general idea of what lies in store for you." My life's destiny is reduced to a small random selection from amongst forty-seven pre-determined phrases.

At best, such practice is an exercise in lateral thinking: it may orient me towards possibilities of which I otherwise may not have thought. At worst, it is a complete denial of self-determination and agency, leading me to believe that I cannot change what will happen to me—only that it may be revealed to me in advance.

Widespread in society, the idea of destiny is as old as the opposing plan in the Council in Heaven.[3] Astrology, horoscopes, oracles, and rune stones are all manifestations of this philosophy. In Roman and Greek times, the "Oracles" were cave-dwelling hermits who gave opium-induced proclamations on visitors' destinies, probably after appropriate payment. Today every popular newspaper carries a horoscope section that many readers religiously follow.

Does a belief in destiny really deny agency? Not if I translate "destiny" as "potential." (Although used in the magazine headline cited above, the word "potential" is curiously left unexplained in the short article.)

The word "destiny" has the same stem as the word "destination." I have a destination—a potential—that I can choose through the way I live. By looking at the way I am living, a wise person could perhaps predict my destination as long as I do not choose to change direction. The scriptures can play this role for me. I can use the Word of God as an "oracle" to help me see my current direction and compare the consequent final destination with my potential. I can then decide whether I like it, and change accordingly.

Some things I cannot change in life, of course. I was born in a particular place at a particular time with a particular ancestry. But I don't believe that such things affect my potential as a son of God. It may be my lot, but not my destiny. "A man can change his stars."[4]

> *Life is like a game of cards. The hand that is dealt you is determinism; the way you play it is free will.*[5]

---

[1] 1 John 3: 2
[2] *Essentials,* IPC Media, London, February 2001
[3] Moses 4: 1-4
[4] Moral from the film *A Knight's Tale*
[5] Jawaharlal Nehru (1889-1964), Indian statesman

55 Chance

To what extent do chance and luck affect my life and my potential? It is certain that no one gains exaltation by chance. For a start, "it is by grace that we are saved after all that we can do."[1] So however lucky I feel, it is through the miraculous atonement of Christ that I am saved, and that Atonement was not wrought by chance, but by deliberate application of agency, by the One whose mission it was, and is, to save me. But still, chance seems to play a role.

In a physics class at school, I remember being fascinated to see under the microscope the jiggling smoke particles buffeted by the surrounding air molecules. The constantly changing balance of collisions on all sides of the particle causes it to make tiny movements in every dimension. On the small scale, the "Brownian motion" of these particles seems entirely random, and yet on the higher scale, order is exhibited through consistent gaseous properties.

I sometimes feel buffeted by the complex combination of events all around me: a car breaking down, a chance meeting with a past colleague, a friend being diagnosed with cancer, a child suffering an accident, a train being late, a change in the weather, catching a cold, or an unexpected business opportunity. These incidents are seemingly random, probably not caused directly by God or any other single agency; they are just a combination of natural events based on the daily, hourly choices of many independent individuals in which God chooses not to intervene. The question is whether there is large-scale order that over-arches this apparent small-scale disorder.

With Paul, I share a basic expression of faith: "we know that all things work together for good to them that love God."[2] This aspect of my faith compensates for the small-scale uncertainties that daily surround me, and gives me confidence that, on the large-scale, my Father in Heaven is ultimately in control.

Language of the Spirit

We cannot direct the wind but we can adjust the sails.[3]

Unlike those passive particles of smoke in the laboratory, I can actively choose how to react to the vicissitudes of life, so often unfair and seemingly random. While it may be a mistake for me to attribute every piece of good fortune to the direct intervention of a loving God on my behalf, it is essential to cultivate a continual sense of gratitude for the good that comes my way. I must remember, though, that God "maketh his sun to rise on the evil and on the good, and sendeth rain on the just and on the unjust."[4]

---

[1] 2 Nephi 25: 23

[2] Romans 8: 28 (See also Doctrine and Covenants 90: 24; Doctrine and Covenants 98: 3.)

[3] Author unknown

[4] Matthew 5: 45

56 Truth

Once upon a time a king gathered some blind men about an elephant and asked them to tell him what an elephant was like. The first man felt a tusk and said an elephant was like a giant carrot; another happened to touch an ear and said it was like a big fan; another touched its trunk and said it was like a pestle; still another, who happened to feel its leg, said it was like a mortar; and another, who grasped its tail said it was like a rope. Not one of them was able to tell the king the elephant's real form.[1]

There are many versions of this old parable, which originates from Buddhism or Jainism. Each blind man is partly correct, but each is too quick to make a judgement on the limited exposure to the whole picture. Imagine thinking that an elephant is just a giant carrot, or a rope! Even if they combine their ideas, the resulting carrot-fan-pestle-mortar-rope creature is not going to seem anything like a real elephant. With this distorted vision, how could one possibly envisage an elephant pulling huge tree trunks with massive strength, or playfully spraying water from its trunk soaking a bystander!

Although originally applied to the discovery of the true nature of man, this parable can also be applied to the experience of Joseph Smith. The blind men around him present a distorted view of life based on only a small part of the truth. Just like the others, the Prophet is blind; but he settles the question by asking the one person who can see: the King himself. In response, the King replies that "they were all wrong," that they have "a form of godliness, but they deny the power thereof."[2] He then proceeds, over time, to reveal to Joseph the true image of the whole animal.

Sometimes having only a small part of the truth distorts the whole view. With the complete picture, the fullness of power and joy can be understood. Rather than building a church based on a single aspect

Language of the Spirit

of the gospel, albeit true—such as baptism by emersion, or on the principle of the grace of God, or speaking in tongues—Joseph Smith had access to the complete picture.

He who lives beyond the veil, can be a source of light and understanding to me, a poor blind man, groping in the darkness. I can know for myself.

> *If any man lack wisdom, let him ask of God, who giveth to all men liberally, and upbraideth not.*[3]

> *When ye shall receive these things, [...] ask God, the Eternal Father, in the name of Christ, if these things are not true; and [...] he will manifest the truth of it unto you, by the power of the Holy Ghost.*[4]

---

[1] *The Teaching of Buddha*, Bukkyo Dendo Kyokai, DHARMA Chapter Three, II 6.
[2] Joseph Smith—History 1: 19. See also 2 Timothy 3: 5.
[3] James 1: 5
[4] Moroni 10: 4

Language of the Spirit

57 Light and Air

The Lord directs the brother of Jared, Mahonri Moriancumur, to build barges to carry him and his people to their promised land. In the process, Mahonri describes three problems:

- "There is no light"
- "whither shall we steer?"
- "we cannot breathe".[1]

Each problem is resolved in a different way. To solve the problem of air to breathe, the Lord proposes an immediate practical solution: a system of holes that can be opened and closed. For the problem of steering, Mahonri is told simply to have faith in the Lord, for the winds will carry them to their promised land. To solve the third problem, however, Mahonri is asked to participate directly. He expends effort in devising a solution, one which nonetheless admits the vital assistance of the Lord—"touch these stones, O Lord, with thy finger."[2]

Imagine spending nearly a year cocooned in a water-tight, air-tight, window-less barge at the mercy of the perilous Pacific Ocean! The journey of this life is also perilous. It takes mankind out of the telestial world (represented by the Tower of Babel, Jared's homeland) to a terrestrial and then celestial world that lies beyond death and resurrection (the Promised Land). The earth is the vehicle, designed to have exactly the right attributes for the survival of its passengers.

By the grace of God I have air to breathe. Breathing is almost effortless. The Lord literally "is preserving [me] from day to day, by lending [me] breath."[3] Spiritual air includes the gift of space[4] for repentance. The conditions of mortality allow the separation of my actions from their consequences, making it possible to learn and develop in faith through imperfection.

I have the wind of the Spirit to fill my sails, and direct me—if I have faith—in the right direction through life. It is my compass, my Liahona.

And I can have light that gives me hope, reassurance, and inspiration. Seeking the light requires a combination of my own creativity—the forging of stones with my hands, heart, and head—combined with the Lord's miraculous touch. It requires me, in short, to live the gospel to qualify for blessings.

> *'Touch my life with light,' we can ask the Lord. 'Fill my heart with hope.' The Lord will do this if we ask in faith and continue to live his commandments. Like the brother of Jared, it is only with the Lord's light that we can see all things clearly.*[5]

---

[1] Ether 2: 19, emphasis added.

[2] Ether 3: 4

[3] Mosiah 2: 21

[4] Alma 42: 4-5

[5] Dwan J. Young

58 Salt

Ye are the salt of the earth: but if the salt have lost his savour, wherewith shall it be salted? It is good for nothing, but to be cast out, and to be trodden under foot of men.[1]

Such has been the importance of salt to human life that the word has crept into many parts of everyday language. The Latin word sal (salt) has survived in salad (salted greens), salami (salted meat) and salary (from the Roman soldier's stipend for the purchase of salt). The related Latin word salvus (healthy or safe) has given rise to salve (healing ointment), salutation (a greeting of good health), salvage (to save) and even saviour and salvation.

Before the days of refrigeration, salt was essential to the cleansing and preservation of meat, fish, olives, cheese, and vegetables. In the Law of Moses, even the "meat offering" (or meal) made from flour, oil, and frankincense was salted.[2] The temple of Solomon contained a "molten sea"[3] reputed to contain some 2000 baths for salting and purification of meat. The temple also possessed a considerable store of salt. Any that had lost its beneficial properties was used to surface the surrounding roads.

Oil, bread, and water are familiar gospel symbols associated with ordinances and covenants. Less known is the Lord's reference to "a covenant of salt for ever unto thee and thy seed with thee."[4] The symbolism is strong: salt stands for incorruption and preservation. It is reminiscent of the permanent nature of the Abrahamic covenant.[5] In the light of this, maybe it is significant that, in both Israel and Utah, God's covenant people are gathered close to great land-locked lakes of salt.

When Jesus says to his disciples "ye are the salt of the earth,"[1] I understand it as a reference to the covenant people of God.

Language of the Spirit

When men are called unto mine everlasting gospel, and covenant with an everlasting covenant, they are counted as the salt of the earth and [...] they are called to be the savor of men.[6]

As an heir to the everlasting covenant, not only does my presence in the population help preserve the whole community,[7] but I have a responsibility to spread the savour of the covenant to others.

---

[1] Matthew 5: 13. See also Mark 9: 49-50.

[2] Leviticus 2: 1, 13

[3] 1 Kings 7: 23

[4] Numbers 18: 19; 2 Chronicles 13: 5

[5] Genesis 17: 7

[6] Doctrine and Covenants 101: 39-40

[7] See how Abraham negotiates over Sodom and Gomorrah in Genesis 18: 23-33.

59 Separation

Come ye out from the wicked, and be ye separate, and touch not their unclean things.[1]

Throughout scriptural history, God has been concerned about preserving His covenant people. They were not to mix or inter-marry with non-covenant makers. For much of the time, His strategy was to *isolate* them from the surrounding population, using techniques ranging from the wholesale removal of the wicked to the spirit world by flooding the earth to the establishment of separate nations—on the other side of the world, in Lehi's case. At other times, His strategy has been to *insulate* them, by teaching living principles that make them a "peculiar people."[2] The saints live among others, but a gospel life separates them in non-physical ways.

In the early days of this dispensation, severe persecution of the saints made isolation necessary. The saints effected a great exodus across the plains to the mountains where they could establish a separate nation. Until 1958, new converts all around the world were encouraged to immigrate to Utah. Then, when the population of the church grew to a certain size, the strategy changed and the gathering place for the saints became their own stakes. Insulation rather than isolation is now the way of life. It is the time when the wheat and the tares are allowed to grow together.[3] I am in the world, but I am not of it.

In the time of Isaiah and Jeremiah, Babylon was the epitome of worldliness and wickedness. "Flee out of the midst of Babylon,"[4] cries Jeremiah, prophesying of its destruction. I wonder what those prophets would make of the goings-on in today's great cities. Today the name Babylon remains symbolic of everything from which the saints should separate themselves. "Spiritual Babylon" is the world and its wickedness.

Go ye out from among the nations, even from Babylon, from the midst of wickedness, which is spiritual Babylon.[5]

Every Sunday, I gather with the saints at church. I isolate myself from the world for a time to help insulate myself for another week. If ever the saints are called to gather anew—to be separate from the world—will I have the courage and disposition to do it? Will I have insulated myself from wickedness sufficiently to be able to recognise the call once more to be isolated from the wicked?

O Babylon, O Babylon, we bid thee farewell;
We're going to the mountains of Ephraim to dwell.[6]

---

[1] Alma 5: 57
[2] 1 Peter 2: 9
[3] Matthew 13: 30
[4] Jeremiah 51: 6
[5] Doctrine and Covenants 133: 14
[6] Hymns of the Church of Jesus Christ of Latter-day Saints, 319

60 Prayer

If you are too busy for prayer, you are too busy.[1]

Too often I forget that prayer is a vital means of preparation. If I am very busy, is it prayer that gets squeezed out first?

Martin Luther King reportedly said that he had so much to do in a particular day that he had to spend half the day praying. The busier I am, the more I should pray. What I pay in tithing is a fixed percentage of what I earn; maybe the amount I pray should be in proportion to the amount I have to achieve.

There are different forms of prayer:

- *Vocal and non-vocal.* As well as vocal, there is "the soul's sincere desire," "the burden of a sigh," and "the Christian's vital breath."[2]
- *Public and private.* In public prayers, one is the voice while others listen, and all are praying together. In private I often pray aloud, even though there is no other human around to hear.

I should engage in all these kinds of prayer, remembering that the real measure of a man is how he lives the gospel when there is nobody around to see or hear. "When we pray alone with God, we shed all sham and pretence, all hypocrisy and arrogance."[3] There is nobody there to impress. It is just me and my maker.

As well as praying in public, I seek the solitude of closet or wilderness to cast my voice to the heavens.

> *When thou prayest, enter into thy closet, and when thou hast shut the door, pray to thy Father which is in secret.*[4]

I need to be where I have no fear of sifting through the innermost secrets of my heart, and expressing them aloud. Untainted by the thought that someone other than my Father in Heaven may be listening, I can, through the Spirit, purchase the preparation of

Language of the Spirit

peace. I am thus shielded against the elements that would spend that peace.

Thus prayer prepares my mind with peace to face whatever challenges the day may bring.

> *And the peace of God, which passeth all understanding, shall keep your hearts and minds through Christ Jesus.*[5]

---

[1] Agnes Gonxha Bojaxhia (Mother Teresa) (1910-1997)

[2] James Montgomery, "Prayer is the soul's sincere desire," *Hymns of the Church of Jesus Christ of Latter-day Saints*, No. 145

[3] Spencer W. Kimball

[4] Matthew 6: 6

[5] Philippians 4: 7

61 Solitude

I will not leave you comfortless: I will come unto you.[1]

Solitude is not the same thing as loneliness. Man is both a social creature—requiring interaction with fellows—and a spiritual being—requiring interaction with God. Loneliness is what I feel when I lack meaningful interaction with others. Solitude is what I seek when I need meaningful interaction with God. Thus I can be alone, but not lonely, and lonely but not alone; I can be lonely in a crowd.

Many of the prophets, including Moses[2], John the Baptist[3] and Joseph Smith,[4] sought solitude for their most meaningful spiritual preparations. The mountains, the desert, and the grove of trees were their places of solitude for personal encounters with God. Even Jesus "departed into a solitary place, and there prayed."[5]

The scriptures teach me to seek solitude in prayer: "ye must pour out your souls in your closets, and in your secret places, and in your wilderness."[6] The Greek word ταμειον ("tameion") translated as "closet" in Matthew 6:6 appears as "chamber" in Matthew 24:26, where it is contrasted with "desert" or "wilderness." Although the closet and the wide-open space seem to be opposites, yet both are "secret places," a means of finding privacy. In the one case I shut the door on the many people around; in the other I go to where there are very few people.

In this day and age, it is hard to find a true wilderness, but it can be done. I like to take a brisk walk on a windy day, and look up at the sky. I see wilderness in the clouds. The upward stance feels like reaching for the heavens, and the infinity of the sky reminds me of His vastness. I will speak a prayer out loud as I walk.

As a student in London, I would often start the day by jogging from my flat in Fulham to Battersea Bridge, where the sky is wide over the Thames. I would lean on the rails in the middle of the river, and watch the reflected lights of the city fade against the rising sun. With early morning traffic passing by, I was not alone. But it was nonetheless my solitude before a busy day.

Maybe it is in solitude that I come to realise that I am never alone. There is an ever-present One who watches after me in love, One who witnesses and understands my every joy and pain, One whose presence is everywhere and inescapable. When, like Joseph, I pray alone and aloud, He hears my prayers.

---

[1] John 14: 18
[2] Exodus 3: 1-5
[3] Matthew 3: 1-3
[4] Joseph Smith—History 1: 14
[5] Mark 1: 35
[6] Alma 34: 26

62 Silence and Solitude

Be still and know that I am God.[1]

Returning from a trip to the beach, my young adult friends and I stopped off in the grounds of the London Temple. Despite there being five of us sardined into a small car, we didn't want to get out, because it was raining. Before we journeyed on, I was asked to say a prayer. "Father in Heaven," I started—then stopped. Because we had been having a rowdy and high-spirited time, I paused for about fifteen seconds to let the Spirit settle into our souls. Quite suddenly, the silence was brutalised by the voice of one of the girls, crying "Don't do that—I can't stand silence!"

I have often reflected on what could possibly being going on in someone's mind for them to be so uncomfortable with silence—so unable to be alone with their own thoughts. Sometimes I seek to shut out irritating noise by closing doors and windows. Other times, I seek refuge from the silence within me by creating noise—by turning on the hifi, radio, or television, by attaching earphones to my personal stereo, or by resorting to the cell-phone. Why do I shy away from myself?

In silence, I face my conscience—the instrument within me that connects to the Light of Christ. To be afraid of silence is to be afraid of the Light of Christ; it is to be afraid of what my conscience is telling me; it is to shun repentance and progression.

Solitude is a vehicle for nourishing the soul. In fact, one might call it "soul-itude." Many of the great prophets—and Jesus himself—sought solitude as part of their spiritual preparation. Alone in the mountains, Moses sees the burning bush.[2] "Finding [himself] alone," Joseph Smith utters his first prayer.[3] In the solitude of the wilderness, Jesus prepares himself for his ministry.[4]

Language of the Spirit

I should seek solitude. I should create the silence my soul needs. I am directed to "pray [...] in private," [5] to "pour out [my soul] in [my] closets, and [my] secret places, and in [my] wilderness."[6]

> *When thou prayest, enter into thy closet, and when thou hast shut the door, pray to thy Father which is in secret.*[7]

In solitude and silence, it is just me and the godhead—the Light of Christ, the Holy Spirit, and Father in Heaven—so intimate and yet so infinite.

---

[1] Psalm 46: 10
[2] Exodus 3: 1-2
[3] Joseph Smith—History 1: 14-15
[4] Exodus 3: 1-2
[5] Doctrine and Covenants 19: 28
[6] Alma 34: 26
[7] Matthew 6: 6

63 Praise

Thou shalt not take the name of the Lord thy God in vain.[1]

One of the principles of lateral thinking[2] is to search for different ways of looking at things. A technique for applying this principle is to consider the opposite of the thing under consideration. I enjoy the exercise of taking the negative commandments—the "thou shalt not"s—and converting them into positives—things I can do. What is the opposite of taking God's name in vain? If I am not to take the name of God in vain, then what am I to do positively with it?

I found my answer in the hymn book. Here is a selection of things I can do with the Lord's name:

Come sing to the Lord,
[...] his name to praise
[...] his name to adore
[...] his name be blessed. (Hymn #10)

Honored and blessed be his ever great name. (Hymn #27)

The world will know the only name
In which the Saints can trust. (Hymn #57)

Shout thanksgiving to his name. (Hymn #61)

On this day of joy and gladness,
Lord, we praise thy holy name. (Hymn #64)

Praise ye his name. (Hymn #67)

Sing the wonders of his name. (Hymn #73)

Exalt his name in loud acclaim. (Hymn #75)

The great salvation loud proclaim;
And shout for joy the Savior's name. (Hymn #90)

> *Teach us how to ever serve thee*
> *And thy holy name revere. (Hymn #150)*

Rather than just refraining from using His name in vain, I can turn the omission of sin into the more active commission of praising, adoring, blessing, honouring, thanking, trusting, exalting, glorying in, singing hosannas to, and revering His name.

I praise his name through song, but also through the way I live. To live the gospel is "to sing the song of redeeming love."[3]

---

[1] Exodus 20: 7
[2] Edward de Bono, author/philosopher (1933-)
[3] Alma 5: 26

Language of the Spirit

64 Order

When God created the earth, He did so by bringing order to materials that already existed. This almost defines what creation is: the reduction of entropy through the introduction of order. Left to its own devices, the world would decay gradually into disorder, greater entropy, a lower state of energy. It requires the constant input of energy to maintain order. Order requires energy and life-giving force.

The word "order" has several connotations: a sense of tidiness or orderliness; a sense of being well-behaved (as in "law and order"); a sense of command (indeed it was by the word of God that the earth was ordered into existence); a sense of method (as in the "order of the priesthood"); a sense of belonging, or being part of an order.

The Melchizedek Priesthood is properly called "the Holy Priesthood, after the order of the Son of God."[1] "Order" in this context seems to mean several things:

- It is the same kind of priesthood that Christ held and holds;
- Nobody holds the priesthood unless they are called (ordered) by God;
- It is commanded and governed by the authority of Christ;
- There is method in its use, for it is "controlled [and] handled only upon principles of righteousness"[2];
- It brings order to the world, not disorder or confusion[3];
- It embodies power; and
- As a priesthood holder, I belong to a brotherhood that spans time and eternity.

As I look around the world, I see a strange mixture of order and disorder. I perceive order in the stars and planets; I admire order in the symmetry and beauty of flowers and fruit. "All things denote that there is a God."[4] But I see death and decay as well; I see the consequences of chaos in people's lives; I see the effects of mortality. God has temporally transferred the responsibility to man, for his own good, to maintain order on the earth, saying to Adam, "cursed is the ground for thy sake; [...] in the sweat of thy face shalt thou eat bread [...] for dust thou art, and unto dust shalt thou return."[5]

I know from my own experience that spirituality comes, in part, from a consciousness of order in my life. I believe that orderliness is next to godliness. Maintaining order is an expression of the creative force I have in me as a child of God the Creator. I can create order round me, and I have the priesthood—that great order of God—to help me.

---

[1] Doctrine and Covenants 107: 3

[2] Doctrine and Covenants 121: 36

[3] See Doctrine and Covenants 132: 8

[4] Alma 30: 44

[5] Genesis 3: 17-18

65 Holy Places

> *My disciples shall stand in holy places, and shall not be moved.*[1]

What is the first thing I think of when I hear the phrase "holy places"? In temples the reverence and respect of the people allow the Spirit of God to dwell in abundance. I feel deep peace and contentment there. Then I remember that my home should be like a temple, a place of tranquility where the Spirit can linger; a place of prayer and scripture study; a place where living the Gospel of love comes naturally. And then again I think of my soul, a spirit dwelling in a tabernacle of flesh. "Know ye not that ye are the temple of God, and that the Spirit of God dwelleth in you?"[2]

I realize that, if I strive to live righteously, I create a holy place around me. When I move, it moves with me, because it emanates from the Spirit of God that dwells in me. This is why "the righteous shall not perish"[3] and "need not fear, for they [...] shall not be confounded"[4] or moved from their place of safety. As long as I have the Spirit with me, wherever I am is safe. "Whosoever hearkeneth unto me shall dwell safely, and shall be quiet from the fear of evil"[5] for God "will not suffer that the wicked shall destroy the righteous."[6]

My place of safety also brings gladness, joy, rest, and hope. And there is no holier place than hope.[7]

> *I have set the Lord always before me:*
> *because he is at my right hand, I shall not be moved.*
>
> *Therefore my heart is glad,*

my glory rejoiceth:
my flesh also shall rest in hope.[8]

---

[1] Doctrine and Covenants 45: 32
[2] 1 Corinthians 3: 16, emphasis added
[3] 1 Nephi 22: 19
[4] 1 Nephi 22: 22
[5] Proverbs 1: 33
[6] 1 Nephi 22: 16
[7] Kobi Yamada, American inspirational writer (1977-) (adapted from "There is no place like hope.")
[8] Psalms 16: 8-9 (see also Acts 2: 25-26)

66 Temples

When President David O. McKay dedicated the England London temple on September 7, 1958, he compared the building to a magnificent oak tree standing in the grounds. Today the tree stills stands with a plaque proudly in its trunk, which quotes the dedicatory prayer:

THE DAVID O. McKAY OAK

(Quercus Pedunculata)

Living beauty and inspiration

Great strength and stability

Reaching toward heaven

Responsive to God's sunlight

Casting friendly and comforting shade

Gentle in its contribution to mankind

Unmoved by disturbing winds

To be remembered.

(September 7, 1958)

I love the ritual of travelling to and attending the temple. As I arrive in the car park and step out of the car, I have the impression of pealing off the world; I undress myself of material, man-made things. As I walk through the doors of the temple, I step out of the unfriendly elements into comforting shade and shelter. As I change into the white temple clothing, I step out of society's symbols of status, and make myself equal to my siblings. As I progress through the temple sessions, I reach toward heaven, following Adam through the Telestial and Terrestrial worlds, finally to arrive in the Celestial room. I find that the world has been washed off.

I return home renewed by the beauty, inspiration, strength, and stability of that experience. I will be unmoved by the disturbing winds of the world, and yet moved by the memory of celestial feelings.

I am not surprised to discover, then, that one of the possible etymologies[1] of the word "temple" is from the ancient Greek word "temnein" meaning a sacred enclosure, or a place cut off.

---

[1] Collins English Dictionary, Millennium Edition

67 The Temporal and Spiritual

All things to me are spiritual, and not at any time have I given unto you a law which was temporal.[1]

Trying to separate spiritual things from physical or temporal things is a mistake. They are inseparably connected, and what influences one influences the other. The health of the body affects the well being of the spirit, and the condition of the spirit influences the state of the body.

I learn from the scriptures that man is element and spirit,[2] and that "the elements are the tabernacle"[3] (or temple[4]) in which our spirit dwells. "The spirit and the body are the soul of man."[5] Death separates body and spirit for a time, and "the dead [look] upon the long absence of their spirits from their bodies as a bondage."[6] In my resurrected and eternal state, though, my body and spirit are inseparably connected, allowing me to experience complete joy.

The elements are eternal, and spirit and element inseparably connected receive a fulness of joy; and when separated, man cannot receive a fulness of joy.[7]

Believing that spirit and element are different in nature is even a mistake; everything is made of matter:

All spirit is matter, but it is more fine or pure, and can only be discerned by purer eyes; we cannot see it; but when are bodies are purified we shall see that it is all matter.[8]

It is no wonder, then, that every commandment is spiritual. Those that seem most directly to be temporal—the Word of Wisdom, the Law of Tithing, the commandment to "cease to be idle [...] retire to thy bed early"[9]—have spiritual consequences: "wisdom and great treasures of knowledge,"[10] "the windows of heaven,"[11] "minds [...] invigorated."[9]

Language of the Spirit

I must learn to nourish my being in a balanced way. As one philosopher put it:

> *One must combine the body, the mind and the heart—and to keep them in parallel vigor one must exercise, study, and love.*[12]

---

[1] Doctrine and Covenants 29: 34

[2] Doctrine and Covenants 93: 33

[3] Doctrine and Covenants 93: 35

[4] 1 Corinthians 3: 16

[5] Doctrine and Covenants 88: 15

[6] Doctrine and Covenants 138: 50

[7] Doctrine and Covenants 93: 33-34 (See also 138: 17)

[8] Doctrine and Covenants 131: 7-8

[9] Doctrine and Covenants 88: 124

[10] Doctrine and Covenants 89: 19

[11] Malachi 3: 10

[12] Karl Viktor von Bonstetten, Swiss author/philosopher (1745-1832)

68 Spiritual Rebirth

Have ye spiritually been born of God?
Have ye received his image in your countenances?[1]

When I was a missionary in Antibes in the south of France, my companion and I started teaching the gospel to a young Frenchman. It did not go well. He had a dark and sceptical attitude that we could not penetrate. He was negative about everything, including his country and his prospects in life. During the third discussion, we discovered that he spoke English, and when he did so his countenance was completely altered. He sat up in his chair, his eyes were bright, and he reacted in an entirely positive manner. He explained that he had visited the United States for a few months, and had a wonderful experience there. Speaking English transported him back into that positive frame of mind. This was the first time in my life I was acutely aware of countenance, its nature and effect.

Alma reminds me that God has a countenance.[1] As I strive to become like God, I will begin to adopt his countenance.

This mini-chiasmus appears in Genesis: "So God created man in his own image, in the image of God created he him."[2] I understand this literally, in two senses: firstly, I am a spirit child of my Father in Heaven, and thus I inherit His image, in the same way that Adam "begat a son in his own likeness, after his image; and called his name Seth."[3] Secondly, even though I inherit specific characteristics from my mortal parents, my physical body is of the same nature to that of God's. Many years before Jesus was born into a physical body, the Brother of Jared marvelled at seeing His finger. Jesus explains,

> *Behold, this is the body of my spirit; and man have I created after the body of my spirit; and even as I appear unto thee to be in the spirit will I appear unto my people in the flesh.*[4]

Language of the Spirit

My spirit and my physical body have the same form, and are inherited at birth in the image of God.

Alma talks about a third aspect of God's image, that of his countenance. I do not automatically inherit this part of God's image; I must accept it through spiritual rebirth. Countenance encompasses appearance, demeanour, attribute, and bearing. These things come not by nature, but by nurture. Striving to live the gospel educates my behaviour and attitude, and engenders in me a Christ-like demeanour. The way I think, the way I walk, the way I talk, the way I look, the light in my eyes—all reflect the effect of the Spirit in my life.

To be spiritually born is to give birth to God's countenance.

---

[1] Alma 5: 14
[2] Genesis 1: 27
[3] Genesis 5: 3
[4] Ether 3: 16

69 Spiritual Progression

[...] and their souls did expand [...][1]

Have you ever tried walking the wrong way up a moving staircase? Living the gospel is like climbing up an escalator slowly moving downwards. I have to make an effort just to stay were I am. If I stand still, I eventually find myself back at the bottom.

Progression in the gospel is a *process*—a combination of actions and natural laws that I have to engage in over a period of time. I cannot get there in one step. Growing and learning are both processes; I cannot buy knowledge of French, and be able to speak instantly. I have to be patient, and engage in the process, and gradually perfect myself.

The scriptures document the spiritual growth process as follows:

- "No man receiveth a fulness unless he keepeth [the Lord's] commandments. He that keepeth his commandments receiveth truth and light, until he is glorified in truth and knoweth all things."[2]
- "That which is of God is light, and he that receiveth light, and continueth in God, receiveth more light; and that light groweth brighter and brighter until the perfect day."[3]
- "If thou shalt ask, thou shalt receive revelation upon revelation, knowledge upon knowledge, that thou mayst know the mysteries and peaceable things—that which bringeth joy, that which bringeth life eternal."[4]

John the Baptist witnessed that even Jesus engaged in this process, for "he received not the fulness at first, but received grace for grace [...] until he received a fulness."[5]

Language of the Spirit

There is a downward process too:

- "And he that repents not, from him shall be taken even the light which he has received; for my Spirit does not always strive with man, saith the Lord of Hosts."[6]
- "This thing commanded I them, saying, Obey my voice [...] But they hearkened not, nor inclined their ear, but walked in the counsels and in the imagination of their evil heart, and went backward, and not forward."[7]

The stairway to heaven takes me progressively and forever upwards. I have so far to go! But my Saviour is there to hold the hand that I reach out through prayer. The scriptures are the guiding banister—the "iron rod."

---

[1] Alma 5: 9

[2] Doctrine and Covenants 93: 27-28

[3] Doctrine and Covenants 50: 34 (This echoes words from Proverbs 4: 18.)

[4] Doctrine and Covenants 42: 61

[5] Doctrine and Covenants 93: 12-13

[6] Doctrine and Covenants 1: 33

[7] Jeremiah 7: 23-24

70 Spiritual Sickness

> *For I was an hungred [...] I was thirsty [...] I was a stranger [...] I was naked [...] I was sick [...] I was in prison.*[1]

I think of these words of the Saviour as being physical acts of charity. In reality, though, each of the conditions listed has a spiritual counterpart: there are many who "hunger and thirst after righteousness,"[2] and yet know not what will satisfy them. There are many who are "strangers to God,"[3] "strangers from the covenants of promise, having no hope, and without God in the world."[4]

The spiritual symbolism of nakedness refers to those who have not made saving and protecting covenants. Ever since God made a coat of skins for Adam and Eve in the Garden of Eden,[5] clothing has been a token of the protection that comes from living the Gospel.

Spiritual sickness is rampant. Many people exhibit such severe symptoms that one hardly knows where to start the healing process. Jesus would know how. He went about healing every kind of sickness, without distinction between the physical and the spiritual.

Many are spiritually imprisoned by the chains of this world, through ignorance, habit, and addiction. Alma defines the "chains of hell" as binding him who "will harden his heart"[6] and not engage in the emancipating growth process of the Gospel. The passage refers as much to sharing the blessings of the Gospel with others as it does literally to sharing food, clothing, friendship, and company with the needy. It applies to missionary work as well as to home teaching. It includes every aspect of my ministry and calling.

Preaching in a synagogue, Jesus quoted one of Isaiah's messianic prophesies:

> *He hath anointed me to preach the gospel to the poor;*
> *he hath send me to heal the broken-hearted,*

Language of the Spirit

to preach deliverance to the captives,
and recovering of sight to the blind,
to set at liberty them that are bruised,
to preach the acceptable year of the Lord.[7]

I am called by the Saviour to be a saviour. When called upon, may I be able to proclaim, like Peter, "such as I have give I thee."[8]

---

[1] Matthew 26: 35-36

[2] Matthew 5: 6

[3] Alma 26: 9

[4] Ephesians 2: 12

[5] Genesis 3: 21

[6] Alma 12: 10-11

[7] Luke 4: 18-19. Comparison with Isaiah 61: 1-2 is interesting.

[8] Acts 3: 6

71 Spiritual Survival

> *O all ye that are spared because ye were more righteous [...] will ye not now return unto me, and repent of your sins, and be converted, that I may heal you?*[1]

This scripture is a recipe for spiritual survival.[2] I am not talking best-practice gospel living here; I am talking about the minimum effort that is necessary for surviving the storm. It is all too easy for the righteous to drift. I was touched when a speaker cited the above scripture. They are the words of the Saviour, calling righteousness Nephites to repentance, those who had probably not intended to drift away in the first place.

The Spirit warned me once not to drift. I was going to complain to the bishop about inadequate home teaching, when the Spirit whispered to me, "If you do this, it will take you out of the Church." That was a shock, because it was not my intention to leave the Church!

To survive in severe conditions, a ship cannot just drift, or it will be submerged by the waves. It must maintain power and head into the storm, "workwise with the wind and the waves."[3] Maintaining power in spiritual terms means doing a minimum number of things:

1. Attending church.
2. Reading the scriptures before sleeping every night.
3. Saying at least one prayer every day.

Whether I feel like it or not, I must be there at church—bottom on the seat—even if my head is in the car park. There is strength in just being in the presence of others, even passively. For years I watched one young sister grow up in the ward without ever having much to do with her. I was astonished one day when she thanked me for everything I had done for her. "What have I done for you?" I asked. "You have just been there all these years," came the reply. To paraphrase John Donne, "any man's absence diminishes me."[4] My absence from church diminishes me. Likewise, I must be there for the Lord through prayer and study. Being there exposes me to the influences that help me to repent and be converted. It allows the Lord to fulfil the promise of healing: "[...] that I may heal you."

---

[1] 3 Nephi 9: 13

[2] This is a paraphrase of a talk given by Maggie Ann Punch at the Reading England Stake conference in January 2005. The first person of this passage is her voice.

[3] Doctrine and Covenants 123: 16

[4] The original line from *No man is an island* by John Donne is "any man's death diminishes me." See Meditation XVII from "Devotions on Emergent Occasions."

72 Spiritual Hunger

> *Because thou sayest, I am rich, and increased with goods, and have need of nothing; and knowest not that thou art wretched, and miserable, and poor, and blind, and naked: I counsel thee to buy of me gold tried in the fire, that thou mayest be rich; and white raiment, that thou mayest be clothed, and that the shame of thy nakedness do not appear; and appoint thine eyes with eyesalve, that thou mayest see.[1]*

The material things I possess give me an illusion of security. I am free from physical hunger, cold, and other material wants; yet deep down I feel yearnings that I misinterpret. In a vain attempt to cure them, I eat or drink or bathe myself in some material solution, not realising that what I suffer is a profound spiritual home-sickness.

If only I could realise that those deep-rooted insecurities cannot be answered by material things; that material things cannot bring me self-sufficiency; that part of my being is a spirit whose origin is elsewhere and whose needs go beyond the material. In this life I cannot be self-sufficient; I will always depend on the Father of my spirit who gave me life, on my Saviour who paid my spiritual debts, and on the Holy Spirit who is my ever-present connection with my spiritual home.

Through the writer of the book of Revelation, the Lord uses powerful symbolism, employing material things as analogies for spiritual gifts. "Gold tried in the fire" refers to those rich qualities of humility, love, and compassion that I derive from the trials of this life. For as He says elsewhere, "As many as I love, I rebuke and chasten."[2] "White raiment" is emblematic of the covenants with which I clothe myself, that protect me from the adverse spiritual climate of this world. "Eyesalve" symbolises the light and understanding that come to me through study and practice of the word of God.

Language of the Spirit

Fasting is a very real way to remember that my needs are more than material. I go without food for a short twenty-four hours—an abstinence that can hardly do me harm. When I feel hungry, I turn to prayer and the scriptures for nourishment. And it works. The pangs are appeased, for my needs are as much spiritual as physical.

When deep yearnings rise to the surface of my consciousness, I must learn to recognise that every physical manifestation is associated with an underlying spiritual need, and that treating such pangs by material means alone may aggravate rather than assuage the basic spiritual pain.

---

[1] Revelation 3: 17-18
[2] Revelation 3: 19

73 Spiritual Debt

God does not expect me to succeed. He expects me to do my best.[1]

When Jesus brackets a story with "the kingdom of heaven is likened unto [...]" and "so likewise shall my heavenly Father do [...]",[2] it is not difficult to ascertain that He is drawing an analogy between natural reality and spiritual reality. I would like to mention two such parables that provide monetary analogies of the grace of God to man.

The first is the parable of the "unmerciful servant"[3] who owes his master 10,000 talents, and pleads for mercy when the debt is due. Although the master's forgiveness is complete, it is not totally unconditional; it is retracted when the man fails to show similar mercy to a fellow servant who owes him only 100 pence, a tiny debt by comparison.

I am the servant. The debt of 10,000 talents is so huge, it might as well be infinite. It represents the infinite demands of perfection required of me if I wish to return to God's presence. No mortal is capable of meeting these demands. Fortunately, our Master has forgiven me the debt by paying it for me. In place of the huge debt, our Master expects new things of me—at least to strive for His perfection, even if in reality I cannot attain it. Part of this is to show similar mercy to those who owe me.

The second reference is the parable of "the talents."[4] In this case, the master gives a different sum of money to each of three servants, and takes account of their efforts when he returns from a long journey. The large sums given out involve great, but differing, responsibility. One of the servants is so frightened by this that he does not even try to do his duty. The efforts of the other two servants, however, are completely accepted by the master, even though he had different expectations of them.

Language of the Spirit

This is about doing the best I can. My best is not the same as that of other people; but that does not matter in the eyes of the Lord. Each will be judged accordingly to their own lot.

These parables teach me that the Atonement replaces what is impossible for me by what is possible. It removes from me the burden of having to be absolutely perfect—the infinite debt—and replaces it by the responsibility to do the best I can—to magnify the responsibilities that are mine. I cannot be absolutely perfect; but I can do my very best. If I do my very best, "then is his grace sufficient for [me], that by his grace [I] may be perfect in Christ."[5]

---

[1] Agnes Gonxha Bojaxhia (Mother Teresa, 1910-1997), when told that she could never succeed in her work to help the poor.

[2] E.g. Matthew 18: 23, 35

[3] Matthew 18: 23-35

[4] Matthew 25: 14-30

[5] Moroni 10: 33

74 Seeds of Every Kind

And it came to pass that we had gathered together all manner of seeds of every kind, both of grain of every kind, and also the seeds of fruit of every kind.[1]

The eighth chapter of First Nephi—which tells of Lehi's vision of the Tree of Life—starts by talking about seeds and has remarkable parallels to Jesus' "parable of the sower." [2] Both talk of four kinds of people who hear the word of the gospel, but have different reactions, as enumerated in the following table.

Lehi's vision	**Parable of sower**	**Jesus' interpretation**
Those who commence the path, but get lost in the mist of darkness.[3]	Those who fall by the wayside, and are devoured by birds.[4]	Those who hear the word, but are then caught away by the wicked one.[5]
Those who eat of the fruit, but are ashamed at those that were scoffing at them.[6]	Those who fall on stony ground, sprout, but are soon withered by the sun.[7]	Those who hear the word, but are offended by persecution.[8]
Those who feel towards the great and spacious building, and drown in the depths.[9]	Those who fall among thorns, which choke them.[10]	Those who hear the word, but get caught up in the cares of the world.[11]
Those who eat the fruit of the tree, and stay.[12]	Those who fall on good ground, and bear fruit.[13]	Those who hear the word, understand it, and bear fruit.[14]

The gospel does not come to me in one sowing. I must constantly prepare the ground of my heart to be fertile to the next visit of the sower. The interpretation of Lehi's vision revealed to Nephi[15] reminds me that the word of God—the scriptures and the study of them—is crucial preparation. It will grant me light to guide me through the dark mists of worldliness, and tools to cut through the thorns of temptation.

---

[1] 1 Nephi 8: 1
[2] Matthew 13: 3-9, 18-23
[3] 1 Nephi 8: 21-23
[4] Matthew 8: 4
[5] Matthew 8: 19
[6] 1 Nephi 8: 24-28
[7] Matthew 13: 5-6
[8] Matthew 8: 20-21
[9] 1 Nephi 8: 31-32
[10] Matthew 13: 7
[11] Matthew 13: 22
[12] 1 Nephi 8: 30
[13] Matthew 13: 8
[14] Matthew 13: 23
[15] 1 Nephi 11: 25

75 Balance

While on holiday in the town of Annecy, France, my family stopped to watch a marvellous street performer. He climbed onto a mono-cycle, and had people from the crowd throw burning batons to him, which he juggled. He managed four at once. Riding a mono-cycle requires good balance at the best of times. But to do it while also juggling four burning batons is quite a trick. But in my experience that is exactly what many people are doing day in and day out. Take mothers, for instance: their burning batons typically include children, husband (usually counts as another child), housework, shopping, church callings, and work. That too is quite a balancing act.

There is plenty of advice around about getting the right balance in life. But the last thing I need is another burning baton thrown at me. What I need are principles to understand and follow, for rather than adding to my burden, they ease it by giving me the space and confidence to make an informed choice. So here are five principles for finding balance in life:

1. *Realising I am unique.* Every person is different. What is right for you may not be right for me. When finding balance, I must have the courage to make choices that are right for who I am. The Lord recognises this. Remember the parable of the talents,[1] and Mary and Martha.[2] Every person must choose the balance of acts that best match his or her capabilities and talents.
2. *Remembering I am a soul.* I have a spirit, a mind, a heart; a balanced diet must nourish all parts of my being. A well-balanced soul-diet includes a daily intake of prayer (for the spirit), study (for the mind) and love (for the heart).
3. *Finding the right rhythms.* "To every thing there is a time and a season."[3] Some things have to be balanced from day to day, such as nourishment of the soul; but others can wait.

Language of the Spirit

They can be balanced over the week, month, year or lifetime. For instance, pursuing family history or engaging in time-consuming further education might just have to wait until the children have grown up a little.

4. ***Not judging myself by the world.*** Many of the things I choose to do are not valued by the world. This is because society does not recognise the eternal importance of, for example, the soul or the family. I must maintain an eternal perspective to stay in balance.

5. ***Having the Spirit with me.*** This is the over-arching principle. If there is no room in my life for the Spirit, then my life is out of balance. The Spirit can reassure of what is right for me, and to choose it at the right time in the right way. Having the Spirit confirms that I am feeding my soul. It helps me keep an eternal perspective. In fact, the Spirit is my very sense of balance. It helps me stay on the mono-cycle.

---

[1] Matthew 25: 14-30

[2] Luke 10: 38-41 (what was right for Mary was not right for Martha)

[3] Ecclesiastes 3: 1

76 Perspective

Survey large fields;
cultivate small gardens.

We used to live behind a small hill that offered a fine vista of the surrounding country. If the view from the top was not particularly breath-taking, the climb up the steep path certainly was! From the top I could see the lay of the land, divided neatly into individual fields coloured by their manner of cultivation. I could see my own house, and how it lay in relation to the other buildings in the village.

As a bishop, I would sometimes walk individuals up there for a talk, usually to help them get their life into some kind of perspective.

The broad view, the wider perspective, is important. It helps me place my life and role in context. Significantly so, the great visions accorded to many of the prophets—Nephi, Moses, Enoch, Abraham—present great vistas of the whole history of mankind on the earth, and of the Plan of Salvation.

But once in a while the sheer scale of what has to be achieved can be overwhelming. I recently experienced the feeling of futility in the face of the great Asian tsunami. How could any contribution I could give really make a difference? Take also the growth of the Church: although the Church is growing in membership, it is shrinking in its percentage of the world's total population. It will take a very significant increase in the numbers of convert baptisms worldwide to change this. Similarly, people are dying at a faster rate than we can perform ordinances for the dead. Is it not all futile?

A favourite, frequently cited story tells of a man on a beach. The sand is covered in tens of thousands of starfish stranded by the tide, roasting to death in the sun. He sees an old woman picking them up one by one and tossing them back into the sea. He comments to the woman about the futility of what she is doing—that she can never hope to make a significant impact on the problem. As she picked up one more and threw it towards the water, she said, "it made a difference to that one!"

It reminds of the words of Mother Teresa: "God does not expect me to succeed. He expects me to do my best."[1] I seek to do my best in cultivating the small garden, the part that is my lot, such that it is uniquely mine. Such cultivation includes my own home teaching, my own calling, my own purity of thought, the haven of my own home, the teaching of my own family.

Yes, I need the long perspective. The temple is the Mountain of the Lord, and offers a grand view that helps me reposition myself and refocus. But my daily efforts are concentrated on the cultivation of my own garden, free from the feelings of futility that I might be tempted to contemplate.

---

[1] Agnes Gonxha Bojaxhia (Mother Teresa, 1910-1997), when told that she could never succeed in her work to help the poor.

Language of the Spirit

77 Invitation

He inviteth all to come unto him and partake of his goodness[1]

Some invitations you just don't turn down. As a young man I was invited to Buckingham Palace to see my father receive an honour—"Commander of the Bath"—from the Queen. In the days when no part of the royal residence was open to the public, this was the chance of a life-time. I was chauffeured in a big black Bentley from my flat in Fulham to the palace, passing through the iron gates where visitors watch the famous Changing of the Guard from the outside. On the inside I witnessed the ceremony in the ballroom, with the Yeoman of the Guard brass band playing from the balcony.

My wife Yvonne says that the most exciting invitation she has ever received was to meet the President of the Church, Harold B. Lee. He was visiting the London Stake where her father was a leader. President Lee asked to meet the children who were patiently waiting downstairs for the meeting to end. A thrill went right through her when the call came: "Come and meet President Lee!" The living prophet shook her hand, and admonished her always to live by the sermons her father taught.

The Gospel is one big invitation: "Come unto Christ." It is an invitation to "a feast of fat things [...] a supper of the house of the Lord, well prepared, unto which all nations shall be invited."[2] In the parable of the supper that Jesus taught,[3] those first invited each decline with an excuse, exposing their preoccupation with worldly affairs. Offended by this disregard for his hospitality, the Lord of the supper tells his servants to go out and bring in the poor instead. They are prepared to listen and accept.

The very nature of an invitation is such that I am not obliged to accept. Nobody will force me. It is up to me to respond. I can give

Language of the Spirit

excuses. However, turning down the invitation may cause sadness and even offence.

In a similar parable, guests are invited to a wedding.[4] Again, so few come that the invitation is extended to the poor and destitute. But there is a stark reminder that, however lowly, guests must be properly prepared: the Lord has the one who is not properly dressed thrown out. Hence the Lord's invitation to "come unto Christ" is also an invitation to change—not just into the proper attire, but to become clean.

> *And again I would exhort you that ye would come unto Christ, and lay hold of every good thing, and touch not the evil gift, nor the unclean thing.* [5]

This is an invitation you just don't turn down.

---

[1] 2 Nephi 26: 33
[2] Doctrine and Covenants 58: 8-9
[3] Luke 14: 16-24
[4] Matthew 22: 2-14
[5] Moroni 10: 30

78 Discipleship

> *Behold, I am a disciple of Jesus Christ, the Son of God. I have been called of him to declare his word among his people, that they might have everlasting life.[1]*

So declared Mormon in an editorial comment in the book that carries his name. It is a model declaration for every missionary called to bring everlasting life to the children of God.

For an explanation of what it means to be a disciple of Christ, who better to turn to than Jesus Christ himself? He says:

> *If ye continue in my word, then ye are my disciples indeed; and ye shall know the truth, and the truth shall make you free.[2]*

I am a disciple of Christ if I seek after, study and abide in His word; in this way I become free from the constraints of sin.

> *By this shall men know that ye are my disciples, if ye have love one to another.[3]*

I am a disciple of Christ when I have natural and spontaneous Christ-like love for others.

> *Remember in all things the poor and the needy, the sick and the afflicted, for he that doeth not these things, the same is not my disciple.[4]*

I am a disciple of Christ when I have compassion for my fellow beings.

The word "disciple" has the same roots as the word "discipline." To be a disciple is to accept a discipline. Self-discipline lies at the root of living the gospel, and forms the foundation of the freedom promised if I practice the principles taught by the Master.

Language of the Spirit

A full-time missionary knows about discipline. The mission rules create a framework for truly becoming a disciple of Christ, "called of him to declare his word among his people, that they might have everlasting life."[5]

---

[1] 3 Nephi 5: 13
[2] John 8: 31-32
[3] John 13: 35
[4] Doctrine and Covenants 52: 40
[5] 2 Nephi 5: 13

Language of the Spirit

79 The Sacrament

When you come together [...] is it not to eat the Lord's supper? [...] The Lord Jesus the same night in which he was betrayed took bread: And when he had given thanks, he brake it, and said, Take, eat: this is my body, which is broken for you: this do in remembrance of me. After the same manner also he took the cup, when he had supped, saying, This cup is the new testament in my blood: this do ye, as oft as ye drink it, in remembrance of me.[1]

Among the gospel ordinances, the sacrament is special. The Bread of Life himself chose the symbols by which His followers are to remember Him. A variety of names are used for this ordinance. Some are as follows:

The Sacrament. This is the preferred LDS term, found only in the Book of Mormon and Doctrine and Covenants, but often used by other Christian denominations as a more general term.

The Eucharist. Paul reminds us that Jesus gave thanks for the bread before breaking it. The root of the Greek word used by Paul is ενχαριστια (eucharistia), meaning "thanksgiving."[2] The sacrament is an act of thanksgiving as well as remembrance.

The Holy Communion. This name emphasises the idea that the sacrament is a way of communing with God and with one another. To my mind, this is associated with:

The Lord's Supper. There are more tokens in the sacrament than the bread and cup. Significantly, Jesus chose to institute the sacrament at meal time, albeit during the highly important feast of the Passover. Eating together has a strong symbolism associated communion and fellowship.

Language of the Spirit

What do I do when I invite friends round to the house? Sit and eat with them. It is a symbol of two-way friendship: offering and accepting. What do I do before I eat each meal? I pause and give thanks through prayer. Every meal is a kind of Eucharist. The word "companion" comes from the Latin "com-" (with) and "panis" (bread) —literally, someone you eat bread with. Missionary companions should eat together as a symbol of fellowship. Families should eat together—a practice sadly declining in the Western society—as a symbol of unity.

Eating the Lord's Supper together at the sacrament table is profoundly symbolic of the communion of the Saints. The chosen emblems remind me of the Redeemer and His Redemption. Participation binds me to Him, and unites me with my fellow believers.

---

[1] 1 Corinthians 11: 20, 23-25 (JST) (It is interesting that Paul does not mention the contents of the cup.)

[2] This emphasis on the fact that Jesus gave thanks for the bread and wine before eating and drinking is interesting, especially as they are symbols of His physical and spiritual suffering. How often do I give thanks for my trials?

Language of the Spirit

80 Estates

Life before birth is often referred to as the "pre-existence," a paradoxical term, as it suggests that I existed before I existed! The scriptures use the term "first estate." This unusual use of the word refers to a state of being granted to mankind, carrying opportunity and responsibility. The closest dictionary definition is perhaps "state, period, or position in life."[1]

This mortal life is my second estate.[2] It is a time of probation[3] in which my Father in Heaven will see if I am prepared to "do all things whatsoever the Lord [my] God shall command [me]."[4] It is "a time to prepare to meet God,"[5] for when I meet Him again, it will be a time of accounting for how I have lived my life.

I know I passed my first estate, because I am here in the flesh; "they who [kept] not their first estate" did not come here as mortal beings, and thus "shall not have glory in the same kingdom."[6] They were, however, "thrust down" to "[go] to and fro in the earth"[7] and became "the devil and his angels," dwelling as miserable unembodied spirits—half-souls—seeking "also the misery of all mankind,"[8] whose role in Heaven Father's plan is to "tempt the children of men"[9] and provide "opposition in all things."[10]

I learn from the scriptures that my first estate, like the second, was a test of obedience and faithfulness. The spirits chosen for special missions on this earth are variously referred to as "good," "noble," and "great."[11] There are some material differences, however. The conditions are not quite the same:

- My first estate was lived out in the presence of God, whereas in this life I am away from His presence.
- There is a veil of forgetfulness that protects me from a memory of my previous life and serves as a test of faith.

Language of the Spirit

- I am a physical being, a step farther along the road to being a complete soul.
- I experience quite a different degree of opposition in this life, due to the invisible presence of those miserable beings who will never experience a mortal probation.

All four aspects serve to create an environment in which the role of agency is paramount.

Will there be a third estate? All I know is that those who keep their second estate "shall have glory added to them for ever and ever."[12]

---

[1] Collins English Dictionary, Millennium Edition
[2] Abraham 3: 26
[3] 2 Nephi 2: 21
[4] Abraham 3: 25
[5] Alma 12: 24
[6] Abraham 3: 26
[7] Job 1: 7
[8] 2 Nephi 2: 18
[9] Doctrine and Covenants 29: 36-39
[10] 2 Nephi 2: 11
[11] Doctrine and Covenants 138: 55 ; Abraham 3: 22
[12] Abraham 3: 26

81 Immortality and Eternal Life

For behold, this is my work and my glory, to bring to pass the immortality and eternal life of man.[1]

Two terms, carefully chosen for their complimentary meanings, describe the scope of God's purpose for man: Immortality and Eternal Life. At first reading, they may appear to have the same meaning: life without end. But elsewhere the Lord clarifies and differentiates His scriptural use of the word "eternal." Speaking about the suffering of the unrepentant, He tells Joseph Smith: "Surely every man must repent of suffer, for I, God, am endless." What has God being endless to do with repentance and suffering? He clarifies:

> *Nevertheless, it is not written that there shall be no end to this torment, but it is written endless torment. [...] For behold, I am endless, and the punishment which is given from my hand is endless punishment, for Endless is my name. Wherefore— Eternal punishment is God's punishment. Endless punishment is God's punishment.*[2]

Thus "endless" or "eternal" do not mean without end, but rather refer to the owner and nature of the thing: "belonging to God." In this context "immortality" refers to the *quantity* of life, while "eternal life" refers to the *quality* of that life—life like God's, in the presence of God. Some will have immortality, but not life like God's.

The two terms also reflect the nature of the Atonement. I receive immortality by being saved from physical death, that part of the gift of the Atonement given to us completely without conditions: "as in Adam all die, even so in Christ shall *all* be made alive."[3] Eternal life is the result of being saved from spiritual death, and is also a gift from God—"which gift is the greatest of all the gifts of God"[4]—made possible by the grace of God through the Atonement, but conditional

Language of the Spirit

on my own choices and efforts. As Nephi said, "it is by grace that we are saved, after all we can do."[5]

Quality without quantity is vacuous. Quantity without quality is miserable. Quantity with quality is endless joy.

---

[1] Moses 1: 39
[2] Doctrine and Covenants 19: 4, 6, 10-12 (emphasis as in original)
[3] 1 Corinthians 15: 22, emphasis added
[4] Doctrine and Covenants 14: 7
[5] 2 Nephi 25: 23

82 Kingdoms

In my Father's house are many mansions.[1]

How many mansions can you fit into a house? As a student in London, my address was 146 Elm Park Mansions, SW10. Each of the two hundred-or-so "mansions" is a three-roomed flat in an early nineteenth century building. Originally luxurious, mine was very seedy at the time I occupied it. Today they are called flats. The intended meaning in the above passage is "room," and some modern Bible translations of the above passage use this word instead.[2]

Modern revelation has clarified certain New Testament terms[3] detailing some of the "rooms" in "Father's house": *celestial, terrestrial* and *telestial*.[4] All three are domains of glory, but differ in degree. Paul uses the sun, the moon, and the stars as a metaphor to draw the eye skywards and the mind heavenwards. But these names and symbols have further significance.

Celestial means *heavenly*; the celestial kingdom is the kingdom of God, where He dwells and prepares "many mansions" for His children. Represented by the sun, the celestial kingdom is the very source of light, and it shines over its satellites, including the earth and the moon, the terrestrial and telestial kingdoms, respectively.

Despite the *terrestrial* kingdom being represented by the moon, the word means *earthly*. At first this seems odd, because the earth is destined to become the celestial kingdom.[5] However, the symbolism is about comparative brightness; the earth and its moon borrow their light from the sun. The glory of the terrestrial kingdom is borrowed from the celestial. "They receive the presence of the Son, but not the fullness of the Father."[6] Terrestrial beings are ministered to by celestial beings.

Telestial means *far off,* in the same sense as *telescope* ("far seeing") and *telephone* ("far hearing"); this is the kingdom of glory farthest

Language of the Spirit

from the presence of God; distance makes the stars dimmer than even borrowed light. The symbolism here is of fragmentation: those who inherit the telestial kingdom live as individuals, *not* sealed to others by temple covenants, *not* partakers of the oneness of God, and *not* enjoying the eternal family. They exhibit disunity:

> *These are they who say they are some of one and some of another [...]; but received not the gospel, neither the everlasting covenant.*[7]

By contrast, the sun is a symbol of unity, a single source of light, Father's eternal family all under one roof. There are many mansions, but only *one* house.

---

[1] John 14: 2

[2] The Greek word monh ("mone") meaning "abode" is used just twice in the New Testament, John 14: 2 and 23. It is translated in the King James Version as "mansion" and "abode", and in the New International Version as "room" and "home," respectively.

[3] 1 Corinthians 15: 40-41. "Telestial" is not used at all in the Bible.

[4] Doctrine and Covenants 76

[5] Doctrine and Covenants 88: 17-26

[6] Doctrine and Covenants 76: 77, 87

[7] Doctrine and Covenants 76: 99-101

83 Innocent Suffering

The suffering of the innocent is a stumbling block for many people. "If there is a loving God," they are tempted to ask, "how come he allows so many innocent people to suffer?" If there is a God, does he not care? Or is he powerless to prevent it? Can a god that cares not, or that lacks the power to intervene, really be a god at all? Where is the meaning in this kind of suffering?

I know God cares. A deeply moving passage in the book of Moses recounts Enoch's education in this matter.[1] In a panoramic vision, all generations of the Earth are paraded before his eyes. He sees Satan brandishing his instruments of misery and captivity, and laughing. Then, in complete contrast, he is astounded to see "the God of heaven" weeping. "How is it that thou canst weep?" he asks, thinking that the great qualities of God—the merciful creator of the universe, author of "peace, justice and truth"—should somehow place Him beyond the reach of sadness and depression. But Enoch is about to be taught a profound lesson. The Lord explains to Enoch that, although He created man, at the same time He gave men "their knowledge" and man "his agency." He commanded men to love one another, but they chose to be "without affection" and to "hate their own blood." Their wickedness causes the innocent to suffer. This causes a caring God to weep.

However, it seems from this passage that it is not so much the suffering of the innocent that causes "the whole heavens to weep." It is more the misery of the unrepentant wicked that invokes such passion. As Ezekiel reminds me, God has "no pleasure in the death of the wicked; but that the wicked turn from his way and live."[2] Enoch learns that the Atonement of the Chosen one gives those who have caused suffering a second chance to be relieved of their own torment. He understands and weeps himself at the misery and wickedness caused by man's misuse of his agency. He discovers that his "omni-pathetic" God cares deeply, not only about the suffering of the innocent, but also about the eventual torment of the perpetrators.

When he sees in vision the "residue of the wicked" swallowed up in the floodwaters, Enoch is inconsolable.[3] "I will refuse to be comforted," he declares. But the Lord has another perspective. He points Enoch to the ultimate source of comfort, the Son of Man coming "in the meridian of time [...] that all they that mourn may be sanctified and have eternal life," and Enoch's "soul rejoiced."

The suffering of the innocent is never permanent. God weeps over those that are lost forever. It is not without reason that Lucifer, "a son of the morning" (the root "luce" meaning light) fell "as lightning"[4] from heaven to become Perdition (the root "perd" meaning lost). Being neither innocent nor repentant, Lucifer was lost for forever, and "the heavens wept over him."[5]

---

[1] Moses 7:28-41
[2] Ezekiel 33: 11
[3] Moses 7:42-47
[4] Luke 10: 18
[5] Doctrine and Covenants 76: 26

Language of the Spirit

84 Pain

> *Heaven knows how to put a proper price upon its goods.*[1]

It seems that to question the need for suffering is to question the existence of God, for "if there is a meaning in life at all, then there must be a meaning in suffering."[2]

If I perceive purpose in my pain, it is easier for me to persevere. My wife was really encouraged during childbirth by the constant reminder that the pain she was suffering was life-giving pain – it gave her a perception of purpose. Some kinds of suffering have clear meaning. Every kind of worthwhile achievement has its price in pain. Athletes talk of the "pain barrier" that they must work through to reach a high standard of performance. Even though the endeavour may be physical, often the pain is mental. I must pay the price to learn a musical instrument through the sometimes painful exertion of self-discipline.

However, most suffering in this world is not through choice at all. Disease strikes indiscriminately. Millions of human beings are the victims of the unequal distribution of the world's resources, and others die painfully before the age of accountability through the circumstances of their birth. Millions suffer terribly at the hands of a small number of wicked men who misuse their God-given agency to wage war and oppression. Natural disasters account for thousands of other deaths. Many more suffer through witnessing the pains and loss of ones they love.

Finding meaning in such seemingly pointless suffering is far more challenging. A starting point is this thought from the French philosopher Xavier Thévenot:

> *It is a philosophical error to think that the meaning of a certain trial can exist somehow independent of the sufferer. [...] It is for man to give meaning to the things that happen to him, to*

maintain an open mind. The question is not, therefore, 'What is the meaning of this trial?' but 'How can I make sense of my life in spite of the meaninglessness that permeates this trial?'

Faith does not, in the end, eliminate from a Christian's life the feeling that some of life's events remain inexplicable, meaningless. [...] Faith permits one, however, to find again and again and forever, new resources to fight for meaning in life.[3]

Suffering brings it own gifts. As Thomas Paine says, "Heaven knows how to put a proper price upon its goods."[1]

---

[1] Thomas Paine, English philosopher (1737-1809)

[2] Viktor Frankl, Austrian psychiatrist and Nazi camp survivor, *Man's Search for Meaning*, Washington Square Press, Simon and Schuster, New York 1984, p. 88

[3] Xavier Thévenot, "Souffrance, bonheur, éthique", Salvator, Mulhouse, 1990, pp. 28-30

85 The Atonement

For the innocent, suffering in this life is of no eternal consequence; but for those who cause suffering, there *are* eternal consequences if they do not invoke the Atonement in sincere repentance. For them, it *does* matter in the end. This is perhaps why the Lord, in his interaction with Enoch, expresses more concern about the torment and misery of the unrepentant than for the suffering of the innocent.[1]

Christ's atonement not only answers the ends of justice for those who choose to repent, it also answers the ends of mercy for those who suffered innocently. Making reference to Isaiah,[2] Alma explains the broad-reaching nature of Jesus' suffering for me: He takes upon himself my "suffering," "pains," "afflictions," "temptations," "sicknesses" and "infirmities."[3] Why? To help establish his omnipathy: so "that his bowels may be filled with mercy, according to the flesh, that he may know [...] how to succor his people" and so that His arm may be ample,[4] with more than adequate strength to carry us through our trials.

The result of the Atonement is that no human suffering is beyond the reach of His understanding and empathy. "Earth has no sorrow that heav'n cannot heal."[5] No mother can say, "He does not know what it is like to go through the pains of childbirth," and no sufferer can say, "He never knew what it was like to have chronic arthritis." Of course He was not a woman, nor did He grow old; but through the Atonement, He chose to experience all kinds of human suffering, exactly so that they can turn to Him in prayer and draw upon the succour of heaven.

> At Auschwitz, the SS hung two Jewish men and a youth in front of the assembled men of the camp. The men died quickly; the child's agony lasted half-an-hour. 'Where is God? Where is He?' someone asked behind me. As the adolescent was still struggling at the end of the rope, I heard it again, 'Where is God

now?' And I heard a voice inside of me reply, 'Where is He? He is here [...] He is hanging from the gallows.'[6]

It is in these thoughts that I begin to understand that poignant reminder to Joseph Smith: "The Son of Man hath descended below them all. Art thou greater than he?"[7]

It is through the Atonement, then, that the innocent find reconciliation for their unjust suffering. It is through the Atonement, also, that those initiators of innocent suffering can find escape, through repentance, from the eternal consequences of their wickedness. It is through the Atonement that I find meaning in suffering.

---

[1] Moses 7:37

[2] Isaiah 53:4

[3] Alma 7:11-12

[4] Theodore E. Curtis, "Lean on my ample arm", Hymns of the Church of Jesus Christ of Latter-Day Saints, No. 120

[5] Thomas Moore, "Come ye disconsolate", Hymns of the Church of Jesus Christ of Latter-Day Saints, No. 115

[6] Eliezer Wiesel, Romanian author, holocaust survivor (1928-), *Night*

[7] Doctrine and Covenants 122:8. See also Doctrine and Covenants 88:6

Language of the Spirit

86 Condescension

*Knowest thou the condescension of God? [...]
I know that he loveth his children*[1]

This question is asked of the young Nephi just before he is shown a panoramic vision of the life of the Saviour. His response indicates that, even if he does not completely understand the question, he is willing in faith to learn. He has an inkling that whatever the condescension of God means, it is an expression of God's love for his children.

The angel's question points directly at the fundamental difference between Christianity and other beliefs: the idea that the God of this mortal world, the immortal Jesus Christ, chose to be born into mortality, live as a mortal being, atone for mortals as a mortal, suffer death at the hands of mortals, and be resurrected to open the way for mortals to return to immortality.

The verb "condescend" has taken on a negative connotation in modern English. In the context of the scriptures, however, the meaning is totally positive. One definition reads "To act graciously towards another or others regarded as being on a lower level; to behave patronizingly."[2] Two aspects of this definition vindicate "condescension": the use of the word "grace," for God's condescension is surely an act of pure grace towards men; and the root of the word "patronize," meaning "to behave like a father."

God the Father condescends to give his Son out of love for us.[3] God the Son condescends by entering mortality to be with man at man's level: "a little lower than the angels."[4] The prefix "con" in condescend means "with," in the sense of He "descends to be with."

In Paul's words, Jesus "made himself of no reputation, and took upon him the form of a servant, and was made in the likeness of men: and [...] humbled himself, and became obedient unto death, even the death of the cross."[5]

Language of the Spirit

Nephi is right, that the condescension of God is an act of pure love. As he gains an understanding of his father's vision of the Tree of Life,[6] he learns that the tree and the fountain of living waters are a representation of the love of God.

I am inspired by an Exemplar who does not lead from behind; who does not lead from a distance in front; but who leads from amongst man. He stands beside me in my struggles, and carries me in my times of need. Because of His complete condescension, He is "touched with the feelings of [my] infirmities."[7]

Indeed, it is almost as if "the Condescension of God" is one of the very names of Christ. When the Spirit asks Nephi "Knowest thou the condescension of God?" he is in effect asking "Knowest thou Jesus?"

---

[1] 1 Nephi 11: 16-17
[2] Collins English Dictionary, Millennium edition
[3] John 3: 16-17
[4] Psalms 8: 4-6 quoted in Hebrews 2: 9
[5] Philipians 2: 7-8
[6] 1 Nephi 11: 2-3
[7] Hebrews 4: 15

87 The Condescension of God

> *[Jesus Christ] ascended up on high, as also he descended below all things, in that he comprehended all things, that he might be in and through all things, the light of truth;*[1]

Part of the universal Atonement is symbolised by Christ's ascent above all things and descent below all things. In a vision given to Nephi, the word used for his descent is "condescension."[2] As the angel explains the life of the Saviour in 1 Nephi 11, he makes direct or indirect references to the following aspects of Christ's life:

- *Conception* (vv. 18-19). God the Father condescends to conceive his only-begotten Son, as Mary was "carried away in the Spirit."
- *Birth* (vv. 19-23). The humble stable serves to emphasize the complete condescension of God into mortality. As Isaiah says, He is "a tender plant, and [...] hath no [...] comeliness."[3] He does not lie on a feather pillow in an exclusive palace, but on a bed of straw in a less-than-ordinary manger.
- *Baptism* (vv. 26-27). The angel sees condescension here also: "notwithstanding he being holy, he [...] humbleth himself before the Father"[4] in just the same way as I need to. Even the act of being lowered into the water is symbolic of condescension.
- *Ministry* (vv. 24, 28-31). However others treated him, he descended to the level of the people. "He raiseth the poor out of the dust, and lifteth the needy out of the dunghill."[5] Not only did He live among mortals, but His life was the epitome of "good will toward men."[6]
- *Death* (vv. 32-33). Jesus was made "a little lower than the angels [...] that he by the grace of God should taste death for every man."[7] A vital part of the condescension was actually to become mortal, and to die at the hands of mortals.

Language of the Spirit

The condescension of God culminates in the Atonement. In the garden of Gethsemane, Christ descends to my level so completely that not only does he suffer to free me from the consequences of my sins, but "he [takes] upon him the pains and the sicknesses of his people," so "that he may know according to the flesh how to succour his people."[8]

There is no human condition that I can experience that he has not also experienced and overcome in life or through the Atonement. His overcoming has made it possible for me to return home from mortality. That is the condescension of God.

---

[1] Doctrine and Covenants 88: 6. See also John 3: 13.

[2] 1 Nephi 11: 16

[3] Isaiah 53: 2

[4] 2 Nephi 31: 7

[5] Psalms 113: 7 (The whole psalm is about the condescension of God.)

[6] Luke 2: 14

[7] Hebrews 2: 9 (Man is also a little lower than the angels: Psalms 8: 4-6)

[8] Alma 7: 11-12. See also Hebrews 2: 18.

Language of the Spirit

88 Opposition

O sisters too,

How may we do
For to preserve this day
This poor youngling,
For whom we do sing,
By by, lully lullay?

Herod the king,
In his raging,
Charged he hath this day
His men of might
In his own sight,
All young children to slay.

That woe is me,
Poor child for thee!
And ever mourn and say,
For thy parting
Neither say nor sing
By by, lully lulay![1]

It did not take long following the gladsome birth of Christ, with its attendant angelic visitations and prophetic testimonies, for the forces of evil to backlash. Within months, a despot king answered the birth of a single child by ordering the murder of hundreds of innocent babies.

This juxtaposition of events epitomises the opposition-in-all-things nature of this telestial world. At one moment Joseph and Mary are rejoicing, shepherds wondering, and angels singing "Glory to God on the highest, and on earth peace, good will towards men"[2]; then soon after in the same town there are other voices heard, "lamentation, and weeping, and great mourning, [mothers of Bethlehem] weeping for [their] children, [who] would not be comforted, because they [were no more]."[3]

How do I answer these grief-stricken women? Why did the God of goodwill not intervene? What kind of God is it that permits the birth of his Son to be attended by such tragedy?

Two millennia later, I feel sure that those same mothers do at last understand, through being able to cast off the blinkers of this existence and rejoin their babies beyond the veil. They will have witnessed directly the compassion of heaven for such events, and perceived for themselves the reasons for non-intervention. They know of the price that has been paid by the Saviour of mankind for the agency of mankind.

Where was God as those infants were brutally murdered? Weeping, grieving alongside their heart-broken mothers.

True to the principle of condescension, Jesus' life was not exempt from the conditions that all of us experience in this low life. Thus it is the Saviour himself who is able to say:

Be of good cheer; I have overcome the world.[4]

---

[1] Coventry Carol, from the *Pageant of the Shearman and Tailors*, 15th century, sung by the mothers of Bethlehem just before Herod's soldiers arrive.
[2] Luke 2: 14
[3] Matthew 2: 18. See also Jeremiah 40: 1.
[4] John 16: 33

89 Golgotha

Eli, Eli, lama sabachthani? [...]
My God, my God, why hast thou forsaken me?[1]

Gethsemane and Golgotha—the places of "the olive press" and "the skull"—are deeply symbolic of two moments of unparalleled suffering. While most of Christendom neglects the importance of what happened in the garden of Gethsemane, Latter-day Saints tend to underplay the significance of the crucifixion in Golgotha. In fact, both experiences were vital parts of the Atonement.

One consideration reveals the different natures of the two episodes: in Gethsemane, Jesus was strengthened by angels;[2] at Golgotha, He was forsaken even by God his Father.[1] God—especially God the Father—had to turn his back on His Son as part of the Atonement; otherwise Jesus would not have "descended below all things"[3] and His condescension would have been incomplete. He had to know what it was like to be completely forsaken and abandoned. As one modern-day apostle put it:

> *It seems, that in addition to the fearful suffering incident to crucifixion, the agony of Gethsemane had recurred, intensified beyond human power to endure. In that bitterest hour the dying Christ was alone, alone in most terrible reality. That the supreme sacrifice of the Son might be consummated in all its fullness, the Father seems to have withdrawn the support of His immediate Presence, leaving the Savior of men the glory of complete victory over the forces of sin and death.*[4]

The agony of Gethsemane was already beyond human endurance;[5] but it was necessary for Jesus experience every dimension of pain. Hence angels were there to strengthen Him through suffering at its full girth in the Garden, but nobody was present to comfort Him during the agony at its height on the Hill.

Language of the Spirit

In His pain Jesus was driven to ask, like all sufferers, the universal "Why?" indicating the completeness of the desertion, and the fullness of the descent He must have felt. Even the taunts He received while on the cross must have magnified the realisation of abandonment: "He trusted in God; let him deliver him now!"[6]

Jesus received no special treatment. Neither the Son nor the Father invoked their unique relationship in the ultimate fulfilment of His mission. He was born a man, He lived as a man, and He died as a man, alone, in Golgotha.[7]

---

[1] Matthew 27: 46

[2] Luke 22: 43

[3] Doctrine and Covenants 88: 6

[4] James E. Talmage (1862-1933), Apostle of the Church of Jesus Christ of Latter-day Saints, *Jesus the Christ,* Deseret Book Company, p. 613

[5] Mosiah 3: 7

[6] Matthew 27: 43

[7] See Hebrews 2: 16-17

Language of the Spirit

90 Bitter Cup

There is a tradition in England at Christmas to drink mulled wine. A variety of spicy herbs, including cloves and sticks of cinnamon, are added to the drink, and it is heated up. My wife makes a similar drink with fruit juices. On the day it is made, the drink is delicious, warming and flavoursome. But the next day, after the spices have been marinating all through the night, the dregs are too bitter to be bearable.

> *In the hand of the Lord there is a cup, and the wine is red; it is full of mixture; and he poureth out of the same: but the dregs thereof, all the wicked of the earth shall wring them out, and drink them.*[1]

The bitterness here probably refers to a similar Hebrew tradition: a mixture of bitter herbs used to flavour wine, and perhaps to make it more intoxicating.

The symbolism is profound. The word "cup" reminds me of the one used by Jesus during the Last Supper when he instigated the sacrament. Paul refers to this as being "the cup of blessing."[2] But the psalmist gives it a dual meaning, variously named as "the cup of trembling,"[3] "the cup of fury,"[4] "the cup of the wrath of God,"[5] "a bitter cup,"[6] and "the cup of [God's] indignation."[7] The context of these scriptures makes it clear that the bitter cup has reference to the justice of God that will be meted out on the unrepentant wicked. The longer the day of repentance is procrastinated, the more bitter the dregs of that cup will become.

The good news of the gospel is that, through His atonement, Jesus has turned that cup of wrath into a cup of blessing. He endured the "cup of bitterness"[8] on behalf of all men. He refilled the cup with the new wine of the new covenant.

Language of the Spirit

Jesus the judge of all pours from one cup, blessing or bitterness. If I apply the Atonement in my life, most surely I will never taste of the dregs, for "my cup runneth over"[9] with blessings.

---

[1] Psalms 75: 7

[2] 1 Corinthians 10: 16

[3] Isaiah 51: 17. See also 2 Nephi 8: 17

[4] Revelation 14: 10; Mosiah 3: 26; Mosiah 5: 5

[5] Isaiah 51: 17

[6] Alma 40: 26

[7] Doctrine and Covenants 29: 17; 43: 26

[8] Matthew 26: 39; Luke 22: 42; John 18: 11; 3 Nephi 11: 11; Doctrine and Covenants 19: 18

[9] Psalms 23: 5

91 Wrath

What must Jesus have looked like when He reappeared from the Garden of Gethsemane?[1] When Judas and the officers came to arrest Him, they did not seem to recognise Him at first, and when He declared Himself, "they went backward, and fell to the ground."[2] And well they might have; for He had been bleeding at every pore,[3] His face must have been stained, and His clothes soaked in blood. He must have looked as if he had been in a wine-press. Indeed, scripture uses this very symbolism: Jesus "treadeth the winepress of the fierceness and wrath of Almighty God."[4] And again, "The Lamb of God hath overcome and trodden the wine-press alone, even the winepress of the fierceness of the wrath of Almighty God."[5] The dye on His garments at Gethsemane is the stain of my sins, for which He chose to face the wrath of God on my behalf. He took upon Himself the wrath of God for my wrong doings, and this "that [I] might not suffer if [I] would repent."[6]

When He comes a second time, our Redeemer will again wear red:

Who is it that cometh down from God in heaven with dyed garments [...]? And the Lord shall be red in his apparel, and his garments like him that treadeth in the wine-vat.[7]

The red garment He will wear at the Second Coming has added meaning. Not only will it remind the righteous that Christ is their Redeemer, who spilt His blood as he suffered the wrath of God on their behalf; it will also warn the wicked that He is their imminent Judge, before whom they face the wrath of God alone. In the words of a well known hymn:

Mine eyes have seen the glory of the coming of the Lord;

He is trampling out the vintage where the grapes of wrath are stored.[8]

Language of the Spirit

How much greater the fierceness of the wrath of the Almighty God must be against those who knowingly ignore the infinite sacrifice made for them! He expends his wrath the first time for all by allowing his Son to be pressed in the vat until He bleeds at every pore. He expends his wrath the second time on those unrepentant people. "They crucify to themselves the Son of God afresh."[9] Notice that it is "to themselves;" they cause and do the suffering.

Red is the colour of wrath. Twice red is the raiment of the Lord.

---

[1] In fact, the word "Gethsemane" means "place of the olive press."

[2] John 18: 3-7

[3] Mosiah 3: 7; Doctrine and Covenants 19: 18

[4] Revelation 19: 15

[5] Doctrine and Covenants 88: 106

[6] Doctrine and Covenants 19: 16

[7] Doctrine and Covenants 133: 46-48 (quoting Isaiah 63: 1-2)

[8] Julia Ward Howe, "Battle Hymn of the Republic", *Hymns of the Church of Jesus Christ of Latter-Day Saints,* No. 60

[9] Hebrews 6: 6

92 Change

They shall be converted, and I will heal them.[1]

When I was serving as bishop, a sister came to me about a troubled relationship with her husband. I had seen them both a number of times, and knew the problems to be deep-rooted. On this occasion, she asked me, "Why can't my husband change?" I tried to reply by saying that that I was working with him, and he needed time. This did not satisfy her. She commented, "When we teach the Gospel to investigators, we expect them to change almost instantly—to give up smoking, and other life-long habits—and many of them do in a very short space of time." She had a point. Ever since that interview, I have wondered about change, why sometimes I find it so easy and instant, yet at other times I struggle over and over again without making any progress. What are the conditions favorable to change? How can we create those conditions?

Maybe I do not really change, but somehow I shed something to reveal a part of my being that was there all the time, just waiting to get out. Michelangelo revealed his hidden masterpieces this way: "In every block of marble I see a statue as plain as though it stood before me, shaped and perfect in attitude and action. I have only to hew away the rough walls that imprison the lovely apparition to reveal it to other eyes as mine see it."[2]

This idea was confirmed to me by an insight from a wonderful book all about the barriers to change:

> *If people are ill, we do not expect them to be transformed into a different kind of physical specimen. We expect them to become as they used to be—healthy or whole (which, incidentally, mean the same thing). They need to feel like themselves again. [...] [Spiritual] transformation does not "make us over" into a different kind of creature, but restores us to that nonconflicted,*

straightforward condition we sometimes call "being ourselves." It's misleading to speak of this transformation as a change. The turnaround moment in the life of the prodigal son, as told by the famous parable, is described in these words: "He came to himself."[3,4]

I do not think of change—and the whole package of will-power, effort, pain, and sweat that seems to come with it—but rather of shedding things that prevent me simply from being myself. The Gospel heals[5] me, and I become myself again. The "re" in repentance stands for "return" to wholeness.

---

[1] Doctrine and Covenants 112: 13

[2] Michaelangelo Buonaroti, Italian Painter, Sculptor (1475-1564)

[3] Luke 15: 17

[4] C. Terry Warner, LDS Philosopher, *Bonds that make us free*, Shadow Mountain, pp. 276-277

[5] 3 Nephi 9: 13; 18: 32; Doctrine and Covenants 112: 13

93 Yokes and Chains

> *Come unto me, all ye that labour and are heavy laden, and I will give you rest. Take my yoke upon you, and learn of me; for I am meek and lowly in heart: and ye shall find rest to your souls. For my yoke is easy, and my burden is light.*[1]

In this beautiful passage, Jesus makes an analogy that appealed perfectly to the agricultural labouring class of His time. What is a yoke? As a carpenter, Jesus had probably made many, and knew all too well how to engineer the wooden frame, gently shaped to avoid chaffing of the neck, that enabled two oxen to pull together in consort, and share their burden.

Jesus' invitation to His listeners, which surely include me, is to share His yoke with Him. He is my partner in the yoke, and by pulling together, my burdens are lighter. The yoke, therefore, is a symbol of the compassion that Jesus feels for us all.

Elsewhere in the scriptures, the term "yoke" is used to symbolise undesirable bondage.[2] This is best compared with another scriptural analogy used for Satan's equivalent: the chains of hell. These also are binding, but they are symbolic of imprisonment, of restriction, of damnation, in which all progress is blocked. No lasting strength comes through Satan.

In contrast, the Lord's yoke, if I accept it, increases my possibilities. My possibilities are increased beyond measure. I can pull burdens that would be insurmountable without Him.

It is also a symbol of the power of covenants. The yoke binds me to Him, and Him to me, just as a covenant is a two-way promise. I accept the yoke through the covenants of the gospel: baptism, confirmation, ordination, marriage. Indeed, at baptism I covenant to strive to emulate Jesus, "to bear one another's burdens that they may be light."[3]

Language of the Spirit

The scriptures also refer to marriage as a yoke. With my wife, my possibilities are greatly increased. Together we share in the Godly attribute of procreation. Together we are able to enter into the covenant of exaltation of the highest degree.[4] It is a yoke for three: a man and wife with the Saviour between them, working together, learning of Him, finding rest to their souls.

I am not afraid to bind myself to the Lord. I know my burdens may not be removed, but the Lord strengthens me through His yoke, and they become light when I share them with my Saviour.[5]

---

[1] Matthew 11: 28-30

[2] Galatians 5: 1, 1 Nephi 13: 5, Doctrine and Covenants 109: 32

[3] Mosiah 18: 8

[4] Doctrine and Covenants 131: 1-3

[5] Mosiah 24: 13-15

94 Mercy

> *There is an odd thing about mercy: by definition, mercy can only be mercy if we don't deserve it. For if we deserve something, then it becomes a matter of justice that we receive it. So it ceases to be a matter of mercy.*[1]

I am so hung up on life having to be fair, that I completely forget about mercy. The whole point about mercy is that it is not fair or just. Mercy buffers me from what, in all fairness, I deserve. Was it fair that Jesus should suffer for my sins? No, it was an act of mercy.

Some of Jesus' parables teach this principle. The prodigal son returns home from a self-inflicted life of misery, and his father rejoices by killing the fatted calf. His brother comes in from working in the fields, and complains, in essence, that it is not fair: he had never strayed and wasted his inheritance, and yet no celebration was made for him. The father's reply: "Son, thou art ever with me, and all that I have is thine. It was meet that we should make merry, and be glad: for this thy brother was dead, and is alive again; and was lost and is found."[2] The prodigal son did not deserve a feast; it was an act of pure grace and goodwill.

A labourer agrees to pay his workers a penny an hour. Some he hires at the start of the day, some towards the end; and yet he chooses to pay them all twelve pence for a full day's work. "And when [the workers] had received it, they murmured against the goodman of the house, saying, These last have wrought but one hour, and thou hast made them equal unto us, which have borne the burden and heat of the day."[3] It was blatantly unfair! The response of the householder to one of them: "Friend, I do thee not wrong: didst thou not agree with me for a penny? [...] Is it not lawful for me to do what I will with mine own?"—justice was not offended—"Is thine eye evil, because I am good?"[4] What a searching question! It is equally applicable to the prodigal son's brother *vis à vis* his father.

Language of the Spirit

How is "the kingdom of God like unto" this? Through His atonement, Christ has put himself in a position to be infinitely merciful in the face of justice. Whatever I actually deserve, my Saviour can reward me with what I truly desire.

This does not excuse me from making an effort, though. The strength of my desire is reflected in how I choose to behave—the way in which I show my love for my merciful Saviour.

---

[1] Stephen E. Robinson, *Believing Christ*, Deseret Book, 1992, p. 60
[2] Luke 15: 31-23
[3] Matthew 20: 11-12
[4] Matthew 20: 13-15

95 Perfection

To think that I am saved by justice is to think that I am saved by works alone. It is to think that I can save myself purely through my own efforts. It is to forget "that it is only in and through the grace of God that [I am] saved,"[1] even "after all [I] can do."[2] However hard I try, I will never measure up to the perfection required by justice. I will always need to call upon the grace and mercy of my Saviour to justify my entrance into the Kingdom of God.

What about the Saviour's admonition "to be perfect"?[3] Note Moroni's understanding: "Yea, come unto Christ, and be perfected in *him* [...] and if ye shall deny yourselves of all ungodliness, and love God with all your might, mind and strength, then is his grace sufficient for you, that by his grace ye may be perfect in *Christ*."[4] It is only through Christ that I can be perfect. And even after loving God "with all [my] might, mind and strength," I still need the grace of God to be perfect in Him.

He goes on: "If ye by the grace of God are perfect in Christ, and deny not his power, then ye are sanctified in Christ by the grace of God."[5] How might I deny His power? By denying the infinite element of grace and mercy in His atonement. I must be careful not "[to have] a form of godliness; but [to deny] the power thereof,"[6] echoing words spoken by the Lord to Joseph Smith in the First Vision concerning churches founded by men.

In the following verse, Moroni talks of "the pleasing bar of the great Jehovah, the Eternal Judge of both the quick and the dead."[7] What is pleasing about it? The mercy wins for me the things I do not deserve.

Why, then, do I repent and keep the commandments? I do it not because I believe that I can succeed purely through my own efforts; rather, I do so as not to "deny the power" of the Atonement. I do it as

Language of the Spirit

an act of love for my Saviour. I do it because that is quite simply the way I receive the gift of perfection freely given.

---

[1] 2 Nephi 10: 24
[2] 2 Nephi 25: 23
[3] 3 Nephi 12: 48
[4] Moroni 10: 32, emphasis added
[5] Moroni 10: 33
[6] 2 Timothy 3: 5
[7] Moroni 10: 34

96 Grace

> *For what doth it profit a man if a gift is bestowed upon him, and he receive not that gift? Behold, he rejoiceth not in that which is given unto him, neither rejoiceth in him who is the giver of the gift.[1]*

Jesus' healing of a blind man is a metaphor of God's grace to man. He rubs moistened clay into the man's eyes, and then tells him to go and wash. Jesus' part is a pure gift of grace; the blind man's part is small in comparison: to obey a simple instruction. The act of washing symbolises his receiving the gift, and helps him rejoice in the Giver.

The Tree of Life in Lehi's vision is placed in the field as a pure act of grace.[2] No payment is necessary to obtain its fruit; only effort is required to reach it, albeit in the face of persecution and opposition. The gift is there; it has only to be received. Assistance is even given to receive the gift, in the form of the Rod of Iron.

There is a famous picture of Jesus knocking on the outside of a door. Close observation reveals that there is no handle on Jesus' side of the door. I have to open it from my side. I have to receive the gift.

> *Behold, I stand at the door, and knock: if any man hear my voice, and open the door, I will come in to him, and will sup with him, and him with me.[3]*

The act of atonement is a pure act of grace. All I have to do is to receive the gift in the way that the Giver has asked: by being obedient to His commandments.

Language of the Spirit

My salvation is a gift. I have only to reach out and receive it. Only then can I rejoice in the Giver.

---

[1] Doctrine and Covenants 88: 33
[2] 1 Nephi chapter 8
[3] Revelation 3: 20

97 Healing

Doctors save lives, prolong lives, and improve lives. But doctors do not heal; they only establish favourable conditions for the body to heal itself. Hospitals are supposed provide an environment suited to healing—although sometimes the home is better.

Preaching the gospel—a life-time healing process—is similar. The missionaries do not convert people; they only establish favourable conditions for individuals to feel the Spirit. In turn, the Spirit prompts them, encourages them and strives with them to live the Gospel. Living the Gospel brings healing, through Christ, made possible by His atonement. The Church provides a healing environment—although a gospel-centred home is also important.

The body's powers of healing often seem miraculous. Spiritual healing also takes a miracle—the Atonement. As Isaiah said, "with his stripes we are healed."[1] Alma says that "he will take upon him [our] infirmities [...] that he may know how to succor his people."[2] The Atonement allows Jesus to ask:

> *Will ye not now return unto me, and repent of your sins, and be converted, that I may heal you?*[3]
>
> *Unto such ye shall continue to minister; for ye know not that they shall return and repent, and come unto me with full purpose of heart, and I shall heal them.*[4]

Note in these verses what conditions are most conducive, if not essential, to being healed: coming unto Christ (requiring faith in Him), repentance, conversion (including baptism and confirmation), and full purpose of heart (enduring in sincerity).

During his ministry, Jesus' miracles of healing the lame, the blind, the sick, and the dead were real, spontaneous acts of compassion. But every one is also a parable of the spiritual healing that Jesus freely offers, as a miraculous act of passion and compassion, to all people who create the conditions necessary for that healing.

> *The greatest miracles I see today are not necessarily the healing of sick bodies, but the greatest miracles I see are the healing of sick souls.*[5]

I have heard someone say, "It'll take a miracle for me to get to heaven!" Actually, the miracle has already been performed. The body can heal itself under the right conditions. Thanks to the Saviour, so can the spirit.

---

[1] Isaiah 53: 5

[2] Alma 7: 12

[3] 3 Nephi 9: 13

[4] 3 Nephi 18: 32

[5] Harold B. Lee, President, Church of Jesus Christ of Latter-day Saints, *Ensign*, July 1973, p. 123)

98 Fullness

> *Blessed are those who do hunger and thirst after righteousness: for they shall be filled.*[1]

"In the beginning [...] the earth was without form and void."[2] The starting point was emptiness. The end point is the fullness offered to the heirs of the kingdom of God.

> *As many as believe in [Jesus'] name shall receive of his fulness. And of his fulness have all we received, even immortality and eternal life, through his grace.*[3]

Other words connected to emptiness are "wane," "vain," and "vanity." They have a common origin in the Latin "vanus," meaning empty or idle. "O the vainness, and the frailties, and the foolishness of men!" says Nephi, "Their wisdom is foolishness [...] and it profiteth them not. And they shall perish."[4]

In contrast to the empty things of the world, the Gospel gradually expands my soul[5] and fills it with the worthwhile things of God. With Mary I sing, "He hath filled the hungry with good things; and the rich he hath sent empty away."[6] Note that, while the Lord may have filled the hungry, He did not take anything away from the rich, for they were empty of spiritual worth when they arrived.

In the Kirkland Temple dedicatory prayer, God is described as possessing "an infinity of fulness."[7] Such fullness does not come all at once. Even Jesus went through the process of growing into fullness, "grace for grace, until he received a fulness." Indeed, there is something about being human that means we have to go through this growth process. Jesus "was called the Son of God, because he received not of the fulness at the first."[8] Keeping the commandments is necessary for me to receive a fulness.[9]

Language of the Spirit

He that receiveth my Father receiveth my Father's kingdom; therefore all that my Father hath shall be given unto him.[10]

Through His love for people, Jesus experienced a fullness of joy with the Nephites: "my joy is great, even unto fullness, because of you."[11] Love is a feeling of fullness, whereas misery is a feeling of emptiness.

Vanity is emptiness; love is fullness.

---

[1] Matthew 5: 6

[2] Genesis 1: 1-2

[3] John 1: 16 (JST). See also Moses 1: 39

[4] 2 Nephi 9: 28

[5] See Alma 5: 9

[6] Luke 1: 53

[7] Doctrine and Covenants 109: 77

[8] Doctrine and Covenants 93: 13-14

[9] Doctrine and Covenants 93: 27

[10] Doctrine and Covenants 84: 38

[11] 2 Nephi 27: 30

99 Life

> *The thief cometh not, but for to steal, and to kill, and to destroy; I am come that they may have life, and that they might have it more abundantly.*[1]

Jesus draws a stark contrast with these words; His mission represents everything that is the opposite of death and destruction; His mission promotes not just life, but the abundant life. "Abundant" comes from the Latin abundantia meaning "fullness", in turn from the verb abundare, "to overflow."

The commandment "Thou shalt not kill" may be transformed into this positive version: "Thou shalt promote life." Promoting life has many facets. Creating life is one: bringing Heavenly Father's spirit children into the world is a way of celebrating and promoting life. Sustaining life is another: advances in medicine and care allow people to live longer. Both of these aspects are about quantity of life. How about quality of life—helping others to live an abundant life and to reach fullness?

The gospel of Jesus Christ is life promoting. It brings an abundant life now, and eternal life in the world to come.[2] Indeed, the most frequent promise given in the Book of Mormon is "inasmuch as ye keep the commandments of God, ye shall prosper in the land."[3] That those who "keep the commandments of God [...] are blessed in all things, both temporal and spiritual"[4] is complimented by these thoughts:

> *From what we get we can make a living.*
> *What we give, however, makes a life.*[5]

> *You are not here merely to make a living. You are here to enable the world to live more amply, with greater vision, and with a finer spirit of hope and achievement. You are here to enrich the world. You impoverish yourself if you forget this errand.*[6]

A good living may be had at the expense of others. The abundant life can only be had for the benefit of others. A gospel-based life is life promoting in every way.

Every time the Spirit speaks, it enlivens me. The language of the Spirit is the language of life and the language of abundance. Rather than dampening my spirit, the Spirit charges me with enthusiasm (meaning literally "God-filled.") Indeed, living in this mortal world, so far from Father's affection, the companionship of the Holy Ghost is perhaps the only way I can sense His presence.

No wonder the psalmist sings "He restoreth my soul: [...] my cup runneth over,"[7] and the prophet cries "see that ye look to God and live!"[8]

---

[1] John 10: 10

[2] See Doctrine and Covenants 59: 23

[3] Alma 36: 1, emphasis added

[4] Mosiah 2: 41

[5] Arthur Ashe (1943-1993), American tennis player

[6] Woodrow Wilson (1856-1924), twenty-eighth President of the United States (1913-1921)

[7] Psalms 23: 3, 5

[8] Alma 37:47

SCRIPTURE INDEX
Bible

Genesis 1: 1-2 194
Genesis 1: 26-27 .... 14, 134
Genesis 3: 5 6
Genesis 3: 17-18 127
Genesis 3: 21 138
Genesis 4: 9 79
Genesis 5: 3 134
Genesis 11: 1 1
Genesis 17: 7 114
Genesis 18: 23-33 115
Exodus 3: 1-5 .... 120, 122
Exodus 20: 3-5 89
Exodus 20: 7 124
Exodus 20: 13 84
Exodus 20: 15 83
Exodus 21: 22-25 96
Leviticus 2: 1, 13 114
Numbers 18: 19 114
Deuteronomy 19: 19 96
Joshua 24: 15 44
1 Samuel 15: 22 42
1 Kings 7: 23 114
1 Kings 17: 14 103
1 Chronicles 16: 29 69
2 Chronicles 13: 5 114
Job 1: 7 158
Psalms 8: 4-6 .... 170, 172
Psalms 23: 3 .... 179, 197
Psalms 23: 5 179
Psalms 27: 4 69
Psalms 32: 2 .... 62, 65
Psalms 34: 18 77
Psalms 46: 10 122
Psalms 75: 7 178
Psalms 111: 10 30
Psalms 113: 7 172
Proverbs 1: 33 128
Proverbs 4: 18 136
Ecclesiastes 3: 1 148
Isaiah 22: 13 90
Isaiah 29: 13 62
Isaiah 29: 16 88
Isaiah 51: 17 178
Isaiah 53: 2 172
Isaiah 53: 4 168
Isaiah 53: 5 192
Isaiah 57: 15 77
Isaiah 63: 1-2 180
Isaiah 64: 8 89
Isaiah 66: 2 77
Jeremiah 7: 23-24 137
Jeremiah 25: 15 178
Jeremiah 40: 1 175
Jeremiah 51: 6 116

Ezekiel 33: 11 164
Daniel 3: 17-18 50
Malachi 3: 8 54
Malachi 3: 10 132
Malachi 4: 5 99
Matthew 2: 18 175
Matthew 3: 1-3 120
Matthew 4: 1 122
Matthew 5: 6 .... 138, 194
Matthew 5: 13 114
Matthew 5: 21-22 84
Matthew 5: 38-48 20
Matthew 5: 41 21
Matthew 5: 43-44 .... 74, 96, 98
Matthew 5: 44-47 57
Matthew 6: 6 .... 118, 120, 123
Matthew 6: 21 92
Matthew 6: 33 72
Matthew 7: 2 99
Matthew 7: 3-5 63
Matthew 7: 12 .... 30, 94, 96
Matthew 10: 22 74
Matthew 10: 28 24
Matthew 11: 28-30 184
Matthew 13: 3-9 146
Matthew 13: 18-23 146
Matthew 13: 30 116
Matthew 18: 23-35 144
Matthew 19: 21 12
Matthew 19: 21-22 92
Matthew 20: 11-12 186
Matthew 20: 13-15 186
Matthew 22: 2-14 153
Matthew 22: 35-40 54
Matthew 22: 39 96
Matthew 22: 40 76
Matthew 23: 27 .... 36, 68
Matthew 24: 26 120
Matthew 25: 14-30 .... 144, 148
Matthew 25: 33 72
Matthew 25: 35-36 138
Matthew 26: 30 178
Matthew 26: 42 42
Matthew 27: 43 177
Matthew 27: 46 176
Mark 1: 35 120
Mark 9: 49-50 114
Luke 1: 53 194
Luke 2: 14 172
Luke 4: 18-19 139
Luke 6: 47-48 30
Luke 10: 18 165
Luke 10: 25-37 30
Luke 10: 31 79
Luke 10: 38-41 148
Luke 11: 39 62

Reference	Page
Luke 14: 16-24	152
Luke 15: 17	183
Luke 16: 13	88
Luke 22: 42	178
Luke 22: 43	176
John 1: 6 (JST)	194
John 3: 13	172
John 7: 17	30, 32
John 8: 7	63
John 8: 31-32	154
John 8: 32	17
John 10: 10	196
John 13: 34	44, 96
John 14: 2	91, 162
John 14: 15-17	53
John 14: 18	120
John 14: 26	7
John 15: 13	45
John 15: 20	75
John 18: 3-7	180
John 18: 11	178
Acts 2: 6	1
Acts 2: 37	32
Acts 5: 41	74
Acts 7: 60	74
Acts 8: 21	72
Acts 9: 4	75
Acts 9: 5	12
Acts 9: 6	32
Acts 9: 16	12
Acts 26: 5	12
Romans 1: 25	88
Romans 7: 18-19	38
Romans 7: 22-23	38
Romans 8: 16	9
Romans 8: 18	26
Romans 8: 23, 25	90
Romans 8: 28	50, 108
Romans 8: 35	75
Romans 12: 14	74
Romans 12: 14-21	98
1 Corinthians 3: 16	128, 132
1 Corinthians 10: 16	178
1 Corinthians 11: 20, 23-25	156
1 Corinthians 13: 12	64
1 Corinthians 15: 22	160
1 Corinthians 15: 40-41	162
2 Corinthians 1: 22	90
2 Corinthians 5: 5	90
2 Corinthians 10: 12	64
Ephesians 4: 13	64
Galatians 5: 1	184
Ephesians 1: 13-14	90
Ephesians 2: 12	138
Philippians 2: 7-8	170
Philipians 4: 7	2
Philippians 4: 9	30
Colossians 3: 1	72
Colossians 3: 5	88
2 Timothy 3: 5	63, 188
Hebrews 2: 9	170, 172
Hebrews 2: 16-17	177
Hebrews 2: 18	173
Hebrews 4: 15	171
Hebrews 6: 6	181
Hebrews 11: 1	48, 90
Hebrews 11: 3	48
James 1: 5	111
James 1: 23-25	29
James 2: 8-9	60
James 2: 14-26	30
1 Peter 2: 9	86, 116
1 Peter 2: 22-23	63
1 John 3: 2	28, 106
1 John 3: 3	28
1 John 3: 5	28
1 John 3: 7	28
1 John 3: 18	30
1 John 4: 20 – 5: 2	44
1 John 4: 21	54
1 John 5: 2	54
Revelation 3: 15-16	79
Revelation 3: 17-18	142
Revelation 3: 19	142
Revelation 3: 20	190
Revelation 12: 1-9	26
Revelation 14: 10	178
Revelation 14: 4-5	62
Revelation 19: 15	180
Revelation 20: 2	100

Book of Mormon

Reference	Page
1 Nephi 3: 7	32, 34, 50
1 Nephi 8: 1-38	146, 190
1 Nephi 11: 2-3	171
1 Nephi 11: 16-17	3, 170, 172
1 Nephi 11: 25	147
1 Nephi 13: 3	184
1 Nephi 22: 16-26	73, 128
1 Nephi 22: 26	100
2 Nephi 2: 9-10	70
2 Nephi 2: 11	158
2 Nephi 2: 14	18
2 Nephi 2: 18	58, 158
2 Nephi 2: 21	158
2 Nephi 2: 26	19, 30
2 Nephi 8: 17	178
2 Nephi 9: 13	10
2 Nephi 9: 15-16	16
2 Nephi 9: 28	194
2 Nephi 9: 42	76
2 Nephi 10: 24	188
2 Nephi 25: 23	105, 108, 161, 188

2 Nephi 26: 33	152
2 Nephi 28: 7	90
2 Nephi 28: 21	78
2 Nephi 31: 7	172
Jacob 3: 11	78
Enos 1: 3	12
Mosiah 2: 17	44
Mosiah 2: 21	14, 112
Mosiah 2: 36	7
Mosiah 2: 38	10
Mosiah 2: 41	196
Mosiah 3: 7	180
Mosiah 3: 19	96
Mosiah 3: 26	178
Mosiah 4: 27	36
Mosiah 4: 29	54
Mosiah 5: 5	178
Mosiah 18: 8	184
Mosiah 23: 17	60
Mosiah 24: 13-15	185
Mosiah 26: 26	36
Mosiah 27: 4	96
Alma 5: 14	134
Alma 5: 9	136, 194
Alma 5: 18	10
Alma 5: 57	116
Alma 7: 11-12	168, 173
Alma 7: 12	192
Alma 7: 23	77
Alma 11: 43	10
Alma 12: 24	158
Alma 27: 27	58
Alma 30: 44	126
Alma 32: 27	53
Alma 34: 26	120, 123
Alma 36: 1	196
Alma 27: 47	197
Alma 39: 8	59
Alma 40: 26	178
Alma 41: 1-15	98
Alma 41: 13	98
Alma 42: 4-5	17
Alma 48: 17	101
Heleman 3: 27-29	34
Heleman 3: 34-35	74
Heleman 8: 25	59
Heleman 12: 6	34
Heleman 13: 19	34
Heleman 14: 31	98
3 Nephi 5: 13	154, 155
3 Nephi 9: 13	192
3 Nephi 9: 20	77
3 Nephi 11: 11	178
3 Nephi 12: 10	74
3 Nephi 12: 19	77
3 Nephi 12: 44	74
3 Nephi 12: 48	188
3 Nephi 18: 32	192
2 Nephi 27: 30	195
3 Nephi 27: 27	28
Ether 2: 19	112
Ether 3: 4	112
Ether 3: 16	134
Ether 12: 4	91
Ether 12: 27	13
Moroni 7: 5-7	62
Moroni 7: 5-9	52
Moroni 7: 16	6
Moroni 10: 30	153
Moroni 10: 32-34	188

Doctrine and Covenants

1: 10	99
1: 11	34
1: 16	88
1: 33	6, 137
1: 35	60
19: 16-17	36
8: 2-3	9
9: 9	9
14: 7	160
19: 4	160
19: 4, 6, 10-11	160
19: 16	180
19: 18	178, 180
19: 28	123
20: 37	77
29: 17	178
29: 34	132
29: 36-38	26
29: 36-39	158
38: 24	77
42: 61	136
43: 24-25	36
43: 26	178
45: 32	128
49: 2	72
50: 24	136
52: 40	154
57: 16-17	82
58: 8-9	152
58: 26	54
58: 28	18
59: 8	77
59: 21	54, 66
59: 23	90, 196
64: 34	36
76	162
76: 5	67
76: 77	162
76: 87	162
76: 94	64

Reference	Page
76: 99-101	163
81: 5	77
84: 38	195
84: 106	77
88: 6	172, 176
88: 15	132
88: 17-26	162
88: 33	190
88: 106	180
88: 124	132
89: 19	132
90: 24	108
93: 12-13	136, 194
93: 14	194
93: 27	194
93: 27-28	136
93: 29	18
93: 30	18
93: 33	132
93: 33-34	132
93: 35	132
98: 3	108
98: 8	16
99: 1	74
101: 35	74
101: 39-40	115
107: 3	126
109: 32	184
109: 77	194
112: 13	182
121: 7	27
121: 36	126
121: 45	64
122: 7	74
122: 8	169
131: 1-3	185
131: 7-8	132
132: 8	126
133: 14	117
133: 46-48	180
138: 8	36
138: 17	132
138: 50	132

Pearl of Great Price

Reference	Page
Moses 1: 39	160
Moses 4: 1-3	14
Moses 4: 1-4	14, 106
Moses 4: 6	50
Moses 6: 56	17
Moses 7: 28-41	164
Moses 7: 37	168
Moses 7: 42-47	165
Abraham 3: 22	18, 158
Abraham 3: 24-25	34
Abraham 3: 25	104, 158
Abraham 3: 26	158
Joseph Smith—History 1: 14-15	120, 122
Joseph Smith—History 1: 19	110

Others

Reference	Page
(Bahá'í) Epistle to the Son of the Wolf 30	94
(Buddhism) Dhammapada (5)	100
(Buddhism) Udana-Varga	94
(Confucianismism) Analects 15: 23-24	94
(Hinduism) Mahabharata, Anusasana Parva 113: 8	94
(Islam) Forty Hadith of an-Nawawi 13	94
(Jainism) Sutrakritanga 1.11.33	95
(Judasism) Talmud, Shabbat 31a	94
(Zoroastrianism) Shayast-na-Shayast 13: 29	94

SUBJECT INDEX

Abednego
   faith of 50
Abraham
   follower of righteousness 73
accountability
   and agency 18
action *30, 32*
   dulled by indifference 78
   fed by feelings 53
   get easier with persistence 38
   responsibility for 20
Adam
   faith of 50
addiction
   reduces freedom 24
adore
   name of God 124
afflictions
   seeking meaning for 104
African tradition
   Golden Rule in 95
agency *14, 18, 22*
   and chance 108
   and destiny 108
   and freedom 16
   and potential 108
   and responsibility 20
   and suffering 26
   having knowledge 16
   having real options 16
   having time and space 17
   price of 26
agricultural
   Jesus' parables appeal to people 184
air *112*
alcohol
   addiction to 24
alliteration
   KJV penchant for 163
Ananias
   afraid of Saul 12
   Paul's first Christian minister 12
angels
   Jesus strengthened by 176
antimetabole
   inner and outer beauty 68
   loneliness and solitude 120
anti-mormon
   Chaplain in the college bar 4
approval
   of parents 40
Aragon
   and Éowyn 24
arrogance
   quality of the ignorant 3
Ashe, Arthur
   quote on life 196
astronomy
   infinite nature 3
atonement *168*
   a miracle 193
   of Christ, and condescension of God 173
   pure act of grace 190
   reconciliation for suffering 169
   refills the cup 178
attitude
   freedom to choose 25
Auschwitz
   concentration camp 168
Babel, tower of
   confusion of language 1
babies
   murdered by Herod 174
Babylon
   spiritual, flee from 116
   symbol of worldliness 116
Bahá'í
   Golden Rule in faith 94
balance *148*
baptism
   covenant of sharing burdens 184
   of Christ, and condescension of God 172
Battersea bridge
   place of solitude 120
beach
   returning from trip to 122
beauty *68*
becoming *28*
being *28*
belief
   transformed by action 30
Benson, President Ezra Taft
   address on pride 76

best
   doing your, shows willingness 36

birth
   of Christ, and condescension of God 172
   spiritual, and countenance 135

bitter cup *178*

bitterness
   cup of 178

Blackwell, Lawanal
   quote about hatred 102

bless
   name of God 124

blessing
   cup of 178

blessings
   failing to appreciate 67
   seeking meaning for 104

blind
   grace of God in healing, man 190
   parable of elephant and, men 110
   still perceive beauty 68

blood
   Jesus soaked in 180

body
   a holy place 128
   muscles get stronger with exercise 38
   physical and spiritual have same form .. 135
   temple of God 128

Bojaxhia, Agnes Gonxha
   death of, compared to Diana 92
   quote about success 144
   vow of poverty 92

bondage
   separation of spirit from body 132

Bonstetten, Karl Viktor von
   body, mind and heart in parallel 133

books
   of Moses 54

boomerang
   and the law of restoration 98

Brigham Young
   scolded by Joseph Smith 32
   test of self-control 32

brotherhood
   of man 56
   of the priesthood 126

Buckingham Palace
   invitation to 152

Buddhism
   Golden Rule in 94
   parable of elephant and blind men 110

Buonaroti, Michaelangelo
   quote about marble 182

burdens
   Jesus lightens 184
   sharing those of others 184
   sharing through yoke 184

candy rock
   lettering an integral part 62
   sold at seaside in Britain 62

captivity
   spiritual 138

carol
   Coventry 174

carpenter
   Jesus made yokes 184

cause
   as opposed to permit 104
   God is not always the 104

celestial
   glory is source of light 162

cell-phone
   refuge from solitude 122

chains *184*
   of hell, spiritual sickness 138

chance .... *108*, **See also luck**

change *182*

charity
   not just physical concern 138

choice *20*
   having real options essential for agency .. 16

Chopra, Deepak
   quote about things multiplying 102

Christ
   invitation to come to 152
   measuring ourselves against 64

Christianity
   condescension of God unique in 170

Christmas
   mulled wine 178

church
   attendance is isolation 117
   provides healing environment 192

cleansing
   with salt 114

closets
    pray in 123
clothing
    coat of skins 138
    symbolic of covenants 138
comedy
    language on the radio 86
commandments
    all spiritual 132
    based on love 54
    expression of love 54
    greatest 54
    lead to freedom 24
    way of receiving gift of grace 189
communion
    eating together 156
    holy, and the sacrament 156
companion
    meaning of 157
compassion
    for fellow passengers 56
    for the unkind 56
    motivates action 31
competition
    a form of pride 76
concentration camp
    Auschwitz 168
    Viktor Frankl 24
conception
    of Christ, and condescension of God 172
condescension *170, 172*
    Christ not exempt from suffering 175
    forsaking of Jesus 176
    no special treatment 177
Confucianism
    Golden Rule in 94
conscience *10, 12*
    faced in silence 122
    Light of Christ given to all 6
    the Light of Christ 122
consciousness
    Spirit communicates at deep level of 1, 8
conversion
    an individual experience 12
    Paul and his conscience 13
countenance *134*
courtesy
    form of gratitude 67

covenant
    of baptism, sharing burdens 184
    salt symbol of everlasting 114
    yoke symbol of 184
covetousness
    a form of idolatry 88
creation
    act of faith 48
    introduction of order 126
    man in image of God 134
    requires life-giving force 126
cup *178*
danger
    brought by bad habits 38
Day of Pentecost
    people ask what to do 32
death
    of Christ, and condescension of God 172
debt *144*
deeds .... *See action*
derision
    the word Raca 84
desire
    and mercy 187
    starting point for love 53
destination
    comparing with potential 107
destiny
    and agency 108
    and destination 106
    and potential 106
    old as heaven 106
Diana Princess of Wales
    death of, compared to Mother Teresa 92
Dickens, Charles
    quote on selfishness **80**
disciple *154*
dishonesty
    cannot be hidden from God 59
    creates anxiety 58
    hall-mark of Satan 58
    heaping up wrath of God 59
    motivated by fear and pride 58
    projecting false image 64
    Satan father of lies 58
    shoplifting experience 58
disorder
    and order in the world 126

doctors
  don't heal 192
dregs
  of bitter cup 178
drinking fountains
  example of extrapolation 100
drugs
  addiction to 24
earnest
  money .... *See* firstfruits
education
  leads to humility 3
egoism .... ***See selfishness***
element
  and spirit 132
elephant
  parable of, and blind men 110
Emerson, Ralph Waldo
  quote on persistence 38
empathy
  and the atonement 168
endless
  meaning of 160
energy
  required for creation 126
enmity
  in contrast to love 76
  manifest as pride 76
  power by which Satan reigns 76
  towards fellow men 76
  towards God 76
entropy
  and order 126
Éowyn
  and Aragon 24
escalator
  walking wrong way up 136
estate 158
  first .... *See* first estate
  second .... *See* second estate
eternal
  meaning of 160
eternal life 160
  not purchased by money 90
ethic of reciprocity See Golden Rule, the
ethic of retaliation
  contrast with Golden Rule 96

  differences with ethic of reciprocity 96
Eucharist
  meaning of 156
evil
  bad habits residue of 38
  knowing from good 6
  propagation of 96
  return evil for 32
exalt
  name of God 124
excuses
  and bad habits 39
extrapolation
  principle of **100**
faith 46, 48, 50
  brings eternal life 90
  brings peace in this world 90
  does not sacrifice the present 90
  fostered by righteousness 91
  helps cope with uncertainty 108
  miracles in response to 5
  story of Chaplain in bar 4
fast offerings
  expression of love 54
fasting
  escape from materialism 143
Father in Heaven
  present in solitude 123
fear
  do not, to be bound to Lord 185
  motivates dishonesty 58
  of Light of Christ 122
  of silence 122
  the righteous need not 128
feast
  gospel is a 152
  parable of the 152
feelings
  are fickle 52
  component of action 52
  component of love 52
  fed by actions 53
fields
  large, and small gardens 150
firm
  meaning steadfast 70
first estate
  devil did not keep 158
  differences from second 158
  in presence of God 158

keeping, precondition for second 158
name for pre-existence 158
test of obedience 158

firstfruits
of the Spirit 90

forsaking
of Jesus by God 176

Frankl, Viktor
quote on suffering 166

frankness
opposite of guile 64

free agency .... *See agency*

freedom *24*
and agency 14, 16, 18
comes from honesty 59
through self-discipline 154

Freire, Paulo
quote on indifference 78

fulness *194*

fury
cup of 178

future
sacrificed for present 90

Gandhi, Mahatma
quote on integrity 62
quote on retaliation 100

gardens
small, and large fields 150

generosity
and greed 83

Gethsemane
and Golgotha 176
appearance of Jesus after 180
place of olive press 180

Gibran, Kahlil
quote on beauty 68

gift
greatest is eternal life 160
must be received 190

gladness
from standing in holy places 128

glass
beauty of stained, windows 68

glory
degrees of 162

goad
hard to kick against 12

prompting of conscience 12

God
agency of 14
in control 108
omnipathy of 164
personal nature of 5
source of all blessings 67

godhead
present in solitude 123

godliness
expressed in order 127

Golden Rule, the *94*
contrast with retaliation 96
contrast with retribution 96
differences with ethic of retaliation 96
principle of action 30

Golgotha *176*

good
knowing from evil 6

Good Samaritan
love in action 30

gospel
a feast 152
an invitation 152
educated demeanor 135
healing process 192
not obliged to accept 152

grace *190*
and beauty 69
gift of eternal life 161
growing in 136
killing the fatted calf 186
not chance 108
saved by, after doing all 188

Grant, Heber J.
favorite quote on persistence 38

gratitude *66*
sacrament act of 156

greed *82*

Greek philosophy
Golden Rule in 94
Isocrates 94

growth .... *See spiritual growth*
catalysed by action 30

guile
and integrity 62, 64, 65
blessed is the man with no 62, 65
opposite of frankness 64

habit 38
Hamsted, Joseph
   regional representative 60
hate
   indifference is opposite to 78
healing *192*
health
   of body affects spirit 132
Herod
   murder of babies 174
hifi
   refuge from silence 122
Hinckley, Gordon B.
   quote on doing your best 37
Hinduism
   Golden Rule in 94
Holy Ghost *6*
   communicates at deep level of consciousness 1, 8
   companionship, principle of balance 149
   language of the Spirit 1
   present in solitude 123
   very sense of balance 149
holy places *128*
   temples 128
Holy Spirit .... *See Holy Ghost*
homes
   holy places 128
   provide healing environment 192
   temples 128
honesty *58*
honour
   name of God 124
hope *46*
   a facet of faith 48
   from standing in holy places 128
   no holier place 128
horoscopes
   and destiny 106
hospitals
   provide healing environment 192
humility
   antidote to pride 77
   comes from gratitude 67
   leads to understanding 3
   quality of the educated 3
hunger *142*
   spiritual 138

hymn
   No. 001 90
   No. 010 124
   No. 027 124
   No. 057 124
   No. 060 180
   No. 061 124
   No. 064 124
   No. 067 124
   No. 073 124
   No. 075 124
   No. 090 124
   No. 115 168
   No. 120 168
   No. 150 125
   No. 240 14
   No. 319 117
hypocrisy
   and integrity 63
   and outer beauty 68
idolatry *88*
ignorance
   leads to arrogance 3
image
   of God, countenance 135
   of God, two senses 134
imagination
   enhanced by knowledge 49
   necessary for faith 48
immortality *160*
immovable
   and steadfast 71
indifference *78*
indignation
   cup of 178
innocent
   suffering of 164, 168
insulation
   in but not of the world 116
   of covenant people 116
   wheat and tares together 116
integrity *62, 64*
intelligence
   and agency 18
   not created 18
   pre-mortal beings 18
   root of agency 18
invitation *152*
   the gospel is an 152
   to come to Christ 152

inward
 motives and outward actions 84
iron rod
 prayer and scriptures 137
Islam
 Golden Rule in 94
Isocrates
 Golden Rule in Greek philosophy 94
isolation
 church attendance form of 117
 necessary due to persecution 116
 of covenant people 116
Jainism
 Golden Rule in 95
 parable of elephant and blind men .. 110
Jesus
 sought solitude for prayer 120
Jesus Christ
 example of equal respect for persons ... 61
 knocks on doors 190
 partner in yoke 184
 seeks solitude to prepare for ministry ... 122
John the Baptist
 witnessed Jesus' growth 136
Joseph Smith
 like blind man asking truth 110
 scolds Brigham Young 32
 utters first prayer in solitude 120, 122
joy
 complete when body and spirit together 132
 from standing in holy places 128
Judaism
 Golden Rule in 94
judgement
 by class and wealth 61
 by the world, avoid 149
 day of 18
 self-assessment 10
juggling
 mother's tasks 148
 while balancing 148
justice
 and the atonement 168
 complemented by mercy 186
 not saved by 188
Karma
 the law of restoration 98
kindness 56
 Christ's, seen as luck 104

kingdoms 162
knowing
 good from evil 6
knowledge
 enhances imagination 49
 of good and evil essential for agency ... 16
Kubler-Ross, Elizabeth
 quote on beauty 68
lakes
 salty when land-locked 114
language 1
 clean and uplifting 87
 colourful 86
 vulgarity and profanity 86
lateral
 thinking 124
Law of Retribution, the
 contrast with Golden Rule 96
lawyer
 questions Jesus 30
leadership
 of Christ 171
Lee, Harold B.
 meeting the president 152
Lewis, Clive Staples
 pride and competition 76
liberty 16
life 84, 196
 gospel give abundant 196
 living to the full 196
light 112
Light of Christ
 different from Holy Ghost 6
 fear of 122
 manifest in conscience 122
 present in solitude 123
literature
 anti-mormon 4
London temple
 dedication by David O. McKay 130
 prayer at 122
loneliness
 interaction with others 120
 is not solitude 120
love 44, 46, 52, 54, 96
 a facet of faith 48
 indifference is opposite to 78
 of God for individuals 5

Lucifer
  plan of 14
luck .... *104, See also chance*
Lyon, France
  missionary experience in 66
mansions
  in heaven 162
Maritain, Jacques
  quote on gratitude and courtesy 67
Markham, Edward
  poem on restoration 98
marriage
  yoke symbol of 185
material possessions
  accumulation of 92
  don't set heart on 92
materialism .... *90, See possessions*
  fasting antidote to 143
  illusion of security 142
matter
  spirit is 132
Maxwell, Neal A.
  quote on bitterness 27
  quote on submission of will 43
McKay, David O.
  dedication of London temple 130
  oak tree in London temple 130
  quote on spirituality 24
meals
  families should eat together 157
  symbolism of eating together 156
measure
  Christ is our 64
  do not, ourselves against others 64
  of our creation 64
meekness
  antidote to pride 77
mercy *186*
  twice blessed 102
Meshach
  faith of 50
Michaelangelo .... *See Buonaroti, Michaelangelo*
mind
  limitation of human 3
ministry
  of Christ, and condescension of God 172

miracle
  atonement a 193
  physical likeness of spiritual 193
mirror
  scriptures like a 29
  shaving without 29
misery
  devil seeks, for mankind 158
mission
  and sacrificing 40
missionaries
  are disciples 154
  do not convert 192
money
  addiction to 24
  cannot buy peace or eternal life 90
mono-cycle
  example of balance 148
moon
  terrestrial glory 162
morality
  Golden Rule essence of 94
Mormon
  editorial comment on discipleship 154
Moroni
  good example of 101
Moses
  books of 54
  sees burning bush in solitude 122
Mother Teresa .... *See Bojaxhia, Agnes Gonxha*
motivation
  action with real intent 52
  and love 53
  inward, leading to murder 84
motives .... *See motivation*
mount
  sermon on the 84
mourning
  mothers of Bethlehem 175
murder *84*
muscle
  will is, of the mind 34
muscles
  of body, get stronger with exercise 38
  of mind, habit and will 38

nakedness
    symbolic of no covenants 138

name
    adore God's 124
    bless God's 124
    exalt God's 124
    honour God's 124
    praise God's 124
    revere God's 125
    thank God's 124
    trust in God's 124

natural man
    reactions of 32

negatives
    converting to positives 124

Nephi
    faith of 50

neutrality
    is usually indifference 78

Nigeria
    Golden Rule in tradition 95

noise
    shutting out 122

nourishment
    of being should be balanced 133

nuclear physics
    infinite nature 3

obedience *42*
    a facet of faith 48
    and sacrifice 42
    demonstrated by action 32
    to God's will 50

Old Testament
    the law and the prophets 54

omnipathy
    of God 164, 168

opposites
    not so opposite 78

opposition *174*
    in all things 158

oracle
    in Roman times 106
    using scriptures as 107

order *126*
    requires energy 126

outward
    actions and inward motives 84

oxen
    yoked 184

oxymoron
    passionate indifference 78

Packer, Boyd K.
    quote on extrapolation 100

pain *166*

Paine, Thomas
    quote on pain 166

parables
    elephant and blind men 110
    of the feast 152
    teach mercy 186
    the sower 146

parents
    approval of 40

Patrick, patron saint
    quote on Christ 87

Paul
    a devote Pharisee 12
    a man of conscience 12
    conversion and conscience 13
    faith of 50
    persecutor becomes persecuted 12

peace
    comes from action 30
    in this world 90
    not purchased by money 90

peculiar
    people belonging to God 86
    people separate 116

Pentecost, Day of
    common language 1

perfection *188*
    and willingness 36

persecution *74*

persistence
    in overcoming bad habits 39

personal stereo
    refuge from silence 122

perspective *150*

Pfeiffer State Park, California
    redwood trees in 71

Pharisee
    questions Jesus 54

pornography
    addiction to 24

positives
  converting from negatives............ 124
possessions... 92
potential.. **106**
  and agency... 108
  and destiny... 108
potters
  Roman, rubbed wax into cracks................62
praise.. 124
prayer... *118*
  at London temple 122
  in private... 123
pre-existence .... *See first estate*
preservation
  with salt 114
president
  of the church, meeting the.......................152
prick .... *See goad*
pride 76
  motivates dishonesty.................................. 58
priesthood
  a brotherhood 126
  an order...................................... 126
  method in its use 126
  rights of......................................73
principles
  ease burdens............................... 148
privacy
  and solitude................................. 120
  pray in 123
  two kinds.................................... 120
process
  definition 136
procrastination
  makes cup more bitter............................178
procreation
  increased possibility of marriage............ 185
profanity... 86
  not beautiful 69
progression *136*
  fear of silence is to shun........................... 122
prophet
  meeting the living.......................................152
protection
  boy saved by Spirit 8
  spiritual, symbolised by clothing........... 138

pure religion
  manifest in action 30
quality
  of life... 160
  of life as opposed to quantity................ 196
quantity
  of life as opposed to quality 196
queen
  of England, invitation to see 152
raca
  origin of word 84
radio
  refuge from silence 122
Rasmussen, Dennis
  propagation of evil...................... 96
  quote about evil.......................... 102
reactions
  actions rather than 32
  of natural man......................................32
reciprocity, ethic of See Golden Rule, the
red
  colour of wrath 181
  worn by Jesus............................... 180
redwood trees
  steadfast...71
reflexivity *102*
  sharing magnifies fulness...................... 195
repentance
  asking what to do leads to 32
  fear of silence is to shun..................... 122
  overcoming of bad habits 38
respect 60
responsibility
  for actions................................... 20
rest
  from standing in holy places.............. 128
restoration.. *98*
resurrection
  free gift to all..................................... 160
retaliation
  extrapolation of 100
retire
  early, spiritual commandment 132
retrogression
  downward process.............................137
revelation *8*
  know for yourself........................111

reverence
   for name of God 125

rhythm
   of life, principle of balance 148

right
   ambiguity of the word 72

righteous
   the, shall not fear 128
   the, stand in holy places 128
   those who live the law 72
   will sit at the right hand of God 72

righteousness 72
   no hard feelings 90
   requires and fosters faith 91

rights
   of priesthood 73

road
   rubber meets the 30

rock
   See also candy rock 62

rod of iron
   assistance in receiving grace 190

Roman
   potters rubbed wax into cracks 62

rowdy
   time, having a 122

rubber
   meets the road 30

sacrament 156

sacrifice 40, 42
   and obedience 42

safety
   brought by good habits 38

salary
   origin of word 114

salt 114
   symbolism of 114

salvation
   compulsary 14
   origin of word 114

Satan .... See also Lucifer
   bound in millenium 100
   father of lies 58
   influences of 24
   no lasting strength comes through 184
   reigns by power of enmity 76

Saul .... See Paul

school boys
   story of, collecting stamps 66

Second Coming
   righteous will survive 73

second estate
   agency paramount in 159
   differences from first 158
   opposition in 159
   out of presence of God 158
   physical body in 159
   time of probation 158
   veil hides memory of first 158

seeds 146

self
   shying away from 122

self-discipline
   brings freedom 154
   makes a disciple 154
   or missionaries 155
   root of gospel living 154

selfishness 80

separation 116

sermon
   on the mount 84

Sermon of the Mount, the
   replacing the Law of Retribution 96

service 44

Shadrach
   faith of 50

Shakespeare, William
   quote about mercy 102

shaving
   without a mirror 29

Shinn, Florence
   quote on Karma 98

shoplifting
   compulsive behaviour 58
   experience 58

sickness 138

silence 122

Sill, Sterling W.
   quote on indifference 78

Simmons, Dennis E.
   quote on life's test 105

sincerity 62
sing
   praise to God's name 124
smile
   giving not like spending money 102
Smith, Joseph .... **See Joseph Smith**
   quote on sacrifice 42
solitude *120, 122*
song
   to praise name of God 125
soul
   body and spirit 132
   nourishment of, principle of balance 148
space
   in life for reflection 104
   to repent essential for agency 17
spices
   bitter in mulled wine 178
spirit *4*
   and element 132
   is matter 132
   separation from body is bondage 132
Spirit, the .... **See Holy Ghost**
spiritual
   and temporal, false separation 132
   growth process 136
spirituality
   a consciousness of order 127
   and freedom 24
stamps
   story of school boys collecting 66
stars
   telestial glory 162
steadfastness *70*
stillness
   God revealed in 122
stories
   car in London 8
   chaplain in the college bar 4
   giving away stamps 66
   short changed 82
   train to London 56
strangers
   to God 138
street performer
   example of balance 148

strict
   and steadfast 71
submissiveness
   antidote to pride 77
subway
   sense of beauty in 68
success
   quote by Mother Teresa 144
suffering *26, 164*
   finding meaning in 166
   of innocent 168
   of Jesus in Golgotha 176
   reconciliation through atonement 169
sun
   celestial glory 162
supper
   the Lord's, and the sacrament 156
survival *140*
symbolism
   of salt 114
Talmage, James E.
   quote on crucifixion 176
tares
   wheat insulated from 116
technology
   addiction to 24
   worship of, is idolatory 88
telestial
   fragmented kingdom 163
   glory is fragmented light 163
television
   refuge from silence 122
temple *130*
   beauty in the 69
   holy place 128
   prayer at London 122
   white clothes in 87
temple, of Solomon
   molten sea in 114
temporal
   and spiritual, false separation 132
Teresa, Mother ...... **See Bojaxhia, Agnes Gonxha**
terrestrial
   glory is borrowed light 162
testimony
   bearing not like spending money 102
   comes from action 30

 comes through action 32
Thames river
 place of solitude 120
thank
 name of God 124
Thévenot, Xavier
 quote on suffering 167
thinking
 lateral.. 124
thirst
 spiritual.. 138
time
 to repent essential for agency 17
tins
 of food, illustrate agency 16
tithing
 and offerings 54
 expression of love 54
 law of, spiritual commandment 132
tobacco
 addiction to 24
Tolkien
 quote on death 24
Torah
 Golden Rule in 94
 the law 54
trappings
 material possessions bind us 92
tree
 David O. McKay oak 130
 oak, compared to temple 130
tree of life
 metaphor for grace of God 190
trembling
 cup of..178
trust
 a facet of faith 48
 in name of God 124
truth *110*
uncertainty
 and faith.. 50
 faith helps cope with 50, 108
understanding *3*
 comes from action 30
unicycle ....*See mono-cycle*
uniqueness
 of individual, principle of balance 148

unity
 and language 1
universality
 and intimacy of gospel 22
unkindness
 negative self-feelings 56
valley
 symbol of steadfastness 70
Veblen, Thorstein
 quote on research 3
veil
 operates in mind 10
Viktor Frankl
 story of concentration camp 24
vulgarity.. *86*
 not beautiful 69
Warner, C Terry
 quote about change 183
Washington, George
 quote on conscience 10
wax
 Roman potters rubbed into cracks 62
wealth .... *See material possessions*
weeping
 of God 164
wheat
 insulated from tares 116
white
 clothes in temple 87
Wiesel, Eliezer
 quote on Auschwitz 169
 quote on indifference 78
wilderness
 pray in 123
will..................................... *34*
 conformity to God's 50
 muscle of the mind 38
willingness................................. *36*
Wilson, Woodrow
 quote on living 196
windows
 knocking on 66
wine
 mulled 178
winepress
 symbolism of 180

Wirthlin, Joseph B
    quote on doing your best 36
Word of Wisdom
    spiritual commandment 132
Word, the
    invites to hear and do 30
work
    addiction to 24
worship
    beholding beauty 69
    gratitude form of 67
    of people, a form of idolatry 88
    of things, a form of idolatry 88
wrath *180*
    cup of 178
Yamada, Kobi
    quote on hope 128
yardstick .... ***See measure***
yoke *184*
Yoruba Proverb
    Golden Rule in African Tradition 95
Young, Dwan J.
    quote on light and hope 113
Zoroastrianism
    Golden Rule in 94

About the Author

Jeremy Dick is a software consultant specialising in information management, with a doctorate in Computing Science from Imperial College, London. He is a convert to the Church of Jesus Christ of Latter-day Saints of over 30 years, and he is currently the bishop of the congregation in Oxford, England, where he lives with his wife and five children. As a young man, Jeremy served as an LDS missionary in Switzerland, where he learnt fluent French. So far, three of his sons have followed his example, serving in Canada, South Africa and Fiji.